Meeting the Brownings

Meeting the Brownings

Michael Meredith

Armstrong Browning Library of Baylor University
The Browning Institute
Southwestern College

THIS EXHIBITION and resulting publication were made possible in part by grants presented to Southwestern College, Winfield, Kansas, from the National Endowment for the Humanities, an independent federal agency, and Baylor University, Waco, Texas, through its Armstrong Browning Library.

PROJECT DIRECTOR: Sandy Feinstein
PROJECT ADMINISTRATOR AND ADVISOR: Daniel F. Daniel
EXHIBITION CONSULTANT AND CATALOGUE AUTHOR: Michael Meredith
EXHIBITION GRAPHICS AND CATALOGUE DESIGNER AND PRODUCTION ARTIST: Christine Lautt
EXHIBITION DESIGNER: Darnell D. Lautt
EXHIBITION AND CATALOGUE PHOTOGRAPHERS: Chris Hansen, Sam McNiel
EXHIBITION AND CATALOGUE CONSULTANTS: Betty A. Coley, Rita S. Humphrey, Philip Kelley

Participating in the exhibition:
SOUTHWESTERN COLLEGE MEMORIAL LIBRARY, SOUTHWESTERN COLLEGE and WINFIELD PUBLIC LIBRARY,
Winfield, Kansas (2–6 April 1986)
ARMSTRONG BROWNING LIBRARY, BAYLOR UNIVERSITY,
Waco, Texas (15 April–17 May 1986)

Published by:

Armstrong Browning Library, Baylor University, Waco, Texas
The Browning Institute, Inc., New York, New York
Southwestern College, Winfield, Kansas

Distributed by:

The Browning Institute, Inc., Box 2983, Grand Central Station, New York, NY 10163

ISBN–0–930252–19–5

Printed in the United States of America by Inter-Collegiate Press, Shawnee Mission, KS
Set in Times Roman type by Wedgestone Press, Winfield, KS

COVER ILLUSTRATIONS:
Front: Drawing Room at Casa Guidi, by George Mignaty
Back: The Lily of Florence
TITLE-PAGE ILLUSTRATION:
The Brownings, by Carol Iselin

CONTENTS

FOREWORD

THIS WORK celebrates the lives and the art of Robert and Elizabeth Barrett Browning. It has grown from an exhibition of letters, books, photographs, and other objects brought together to illuminate the achievements of the Brownings and their friends.

The exhibition and Michael Meredith's graceful catalogue make "Meeting the Brownings" more than a cliché. To meet the Brownings is to discover real people who for most of us have existed only in the reductive imagery of commercials, greeting cards, and classrooms.

Sandy Feinstein, a faculty member at Southwestern College, conceived this project at a 1985 conference in Santa Barbara, California. Under discussion was a joint effort of the National Endowment for the Humanities and the American Library Association for bringing the public into America's libraries. Ms. Feinstein, upon returning to Kansas, enlisted the help of Philip Kelley. A modest exhibition, drawing exclusively on Mr. Kelley's collection of Browningiana and on the work he directs at Wedgestone Press, was designed. A grant proposal was written by Ms. Feinstein and submitted to the NEH.

Confirmation of the success of this application coincided with a visit to Wedgestone Press by Michael Meredith, of Eton College, with a newly discovered item: the earliest known photograph of Robert Browning. From that point and that photograph, the exhibition evolved rapidly to a project which called on the resources of museums, libraries, and private collections in Italy, England, and the United States.

Soon to join the project was Betty A. Coley, librarian of the Armstrong

Browning Library, Baylor University. The resources of the Library were placed at our disposal, and Mrs. Coley worked tirelessly to gather additional items required by the catalogue's narrative design.

With Sandy Feinstein, Philip Kelley, Michael Meredith and Betty A. Coley, I join in expressing deepest gratitude to the individuals and institutions who have placed so many priceless objects in our care.

The continuing support of the National Endowment for the Humanities, Southwestern College, Baylor University, The Browning Institute, Wedgestone Press, and Winfield Public Library was essential to the realization of this exhibition.

We gratefully acknowledge the catalogue's graphic design provided by Christine Lautt and the exhibition design created by Darnell D. Lautt. Also the contributions of Rita S. Humphrey in administration and coordination are sincerely appreciated.

An exhibition of this kind could not be achieved without the generosity and earnest efforts of an enormous number of people. Space dictates the mention only of: Jeffrey Abt, Susan M. Allen, Mary V. Altham, R.J.L. Altham, Anne Anninger, Martin Antonetti, Joseph Arkins, Katherine Armstrong, Anna Lou Ashby, Elaine Baly, John S. Belew, Fredoon Bhote, Bruce Blake, Roy E. Bolton, R.A. Bowden, Sue Bowling, P.A. Bullock, Katherine Cain, John Chalmers, Judith Charlton, Kenneth Coley, Mr. & Mrs. Harry L. Dalton, Carolyn Davis, Nancy Dobbins, Sandra Donaldson, Howard Dudgeon, Clive R. Dunnico, Scott H. Duvall, Donna Elliott, Chad Flake, Joseph Francus, Eleanor Gustafson, Edward Hagan, James Hlad, David J. Holmes, Ronald Hudson, Paul Jackson, Jennie Jennings, David Knott, Gary F. Kurutz, Mark Samuels Lasner, Jennifer B. Lee, Teresa A. Leiferman, Patience-Anne W. Lenk, Scott D. Lewis, Jonathan A. Lindsey, Kenneth A. Lohf, Edward Lyon, Katharine Macdonald, Michael Francis McGraw, Lesley Montgomery, Edward R. Moulton-Barrett, Gordon E. Moulton-Barrett, Thomas K. Myer, Anelle O'Neil, Donald Owen, Frank Patenella, Gordon N. Ray, Judy Harvek Sahak, Phillip D. Sharp, Earl Spidel, Diane Steadham, Karen Summers, Devon Susholtz, Lola L. Szladits, Alexander D. Wainwright, Kay Walker, Kathleen Weibel, Mark F. Weimer, Jack Wernette, Margaret Wernette, Kathy Wilgers, John Willoughby, Edwin Wolf, II, Robert B. Wolf, and A.W. Yeats.

Grateful thanks are also given to John Murray, for permission to quote from the works of the Brownings protected by his copyright.

To all these contributors, and individuals not named but who assisted in this project, we offer this opportunity to meet the Brownings as our response to your contributions.

Daniel F. Daniel, Chairman
Division of Humanities
Southwestern College
Winfield, Kansas

INTRODUCTION

MEETING THE BROWNINGS was a cherished memory for many British and American visitors to Florence in the 1850's. Upon their marriage the Brownings found themselves celebrities, and therefore numerous accounts of meetings survive to tease biographers with a kaleidoscope of impressions. Such accounts—together with photographs, paintings and drawings—are full of half-truths, simplifications, and distortions, for to meet the Brownings was not the same as to know the Brownings—and few could claim that distinction.

Sifting through memoirs and letters by and about the Brownings, and looking at their likenesses, one is aware of contradictions. Those who met the Brownings usually arrived with preconceptions which were either fulfilled or destroyed. As young Henriette Corkran exclaimed in 1852:

> Could that frail little lady, attired in a simple grey dress and straw bonnet, and the cheerful gentleman in a brown overcoat, be great poets![1]

Reminiscences tended to be coloured by previous or subsequent events, and were often written down many years after the encounter. Thus Julian Hawthorne, arriving at Casa Guidi with his parents, was disillusioned by Elizabeth:

> Mrs. Browning seemed to me a sort of miniature monstrosity; there was no body to her, only a mass of dark curls and queer, dark eyes.[2]

A few years earlier another American, the older George Stillman Hillard, received a different impression:

> Her tremulous voice often flutters over her words like the flame of a dying candle over the wick. I have never seen a human frame which

seemed so nearly a transparent veil for a celestial and immortal spirit.[3]

These descriptions, which might loosely be called the grotesque and the romantic, have little value. Hawthorne's dislike of the Brownings is apparent throughout his book, but his prejudiced and exaggerated description is easier to dismiss than the romantic fallacy perpetrated by Hillard, for it is his type of description that is most commonly used by those who met her. The portrait of Elizabeth as an ethereal semi-invalided genius haunts the early biographies. Frail she may have been, but after her marriage she was a more active, motherly woman than the myth will allow, with more wit, sense of fun and love of adventure. A more factual account is preferable to the subjectively romantic. As a girl, Anne Thackeray met Elizabeth in Florence and recorded in her diary:

> She is very small, she is brown, with dark eyes and dead-brown hair; she has white teeth, and a low, curious voice; she has a manner full of charm and kindness; she rarely laughs, but is always cheerful and smiling; her eyes are very bright.[4]

Later she attempted to describe Elizabeth's speech:

> I can remember her voice, a sort of faint minor chord, as she, lisping the "r" a little, uttered her remonstrating "Robert!" and his loud, dominant baritone sweeping away every possible plea she and my father could make.[5]

Neither description gets us very far towards an understanding of Elizabeth's character, but both provide seemingly objective impressions which serve as supplements to the photographs and portraits of Elizabeth made in this period.

There are comparatively few drawings and paintings of Elizabeth before 1850; most are amateur sketches made by members of her gifted family. Surviving photographs date from only three years before her death and show her worn and tired, though affectionately proud of eleven-year-old Pen who shared one sitting with his mother. Her photographs are faithful but disappointing, not for what they show, but for what they fail to show. For a better understanding one turns instead to portraits drawn from life during the 1850's. Of these, the one Elizabeth favoured was that by Field Talfourd. This chalk drawing, which exists in two versions,[6] Elizabeth herself described as idealized. "It may be my spiritual face," she wrote to her sister Arabella. Certainly she looks much younger than her fifty-three years ("rather a transfiguration than a literal likeness"[7]), but Talfourd's drawing conveys a great deal about one aspect of Elizabeth Barrett Browning's personality. Her tender sympathy is there, and her large eyes with their direct gaze suggest intelligence, firmness and resolution. The second version of the picture, that owned by Browning (plate 19), possesses a humanity which gets one closer to Elizabeth than any other visual representation. What it fails to convey is that vivacity and impulsiveness which is so evident in her letters.

There are many more likenesses of Robert Browning than of Elizabeth. They span fifty years. Among the first is the youthful pencil sketch by his friend André Victor Amédée de Ripert-Monclar. Among the last is the sketch by G.D. Giles drawn on Browning's final visit to Italy. By

far the most vivid of Browning's portraits is the earliest-known photograph, by Mayer and Pierson, sent to his American publisher (plate 16). As in all his portraits, Browning adopts a conscious pose. He sits with his right hand resting on his leg in a most contrived position, looking squarely at the camera. Yet for once the pose almost breaks down and there is a sense of restlessness about the photograph. It was taken on 2 June 1856 in Paris, a very hot day, and Browning "literally ran and got done for."[8] His hair needs cutting, his beard is untrimmed and his face betrays a little of the impatience that was so often close to the surface of Browning's character. It is this which distinguishes the early photograph from the paintings by Gordigiani and Field Talfourd and the drawings by Leighton and Lehmann of the same period.

Twenty years before this photograph Harrison Ainsworth, in a letter to John Macrone, also caught a glimpse of Browning slightly off-guard:

> In appearance he might pass for a son of Paganini[,] and Maclise and I must hide our diminished heads before his super abundant black locks—while even your whiskers . . . are insignificant compared with his lion-like ruff. But his is absurd—and, as absurdity is the farthest thing removed from Mr. Browning, I ought not to connect anything of the kind with him.[9]

A little later Miss Eliza Fox was equally perceptive:

> Mr. Browning entered the drawing room with a quick light step. . . . He was slim and dark and very handsome; and—may I hint it—just a trifle of the dandy, but full of ambition, eager for success, eager for fame, and, what's more, determined to conquer fame and to achieve success.[10]

In the mid-1840's Browning was spied at Thomas Carlyle's by Thomas Powell:

> Earnestly talking with another, stands Browning, leaning on the mantlepiece; his well made, neatly dressed figure, of the small size, has a dapper appearance: his sallow complexion garnished with coal-black whiskers, which grow under the chin. . . . He is doubtless pointing out some curious passage from his favourite poet Donne, or quoting with extreme unction a few lines from Kit Smart, the mad poet; possibly he may be explaining some peculiar dramatic effect of Alfieri.[11]

What distinguishes these three impressions gathered over a decade is their similarity. They are obviously speaking of the same person. The slight affectation as well as the intensity of the young Browning is seen through different but kindly eyes. Powell's tone becomes more critical when he begins to describe Browning's erudite conversation ("extreme unction" is a vile phrase, as Polonius would have said), but one feels that in these descriptions one is getting to know something about the man, his vigour and his vulnerability.

During the decade before the Brownings' marriage, while Robert circulated actively in society and thus was readily available for observation, Elizabeth remained secluded in London and Torquay—seen by scarcely anybody except family members. R.H. Horne, in his *New Spirit of the Age* (1844), described her as living in "almost hermetically sealed" surroundings and seeing no one.

Marriage changed both the Brownings' social habits. For much of the time in Italy Robert and Elizabeth led a quietly private domestic life at Casa Guidi—he less in society than before, she considerably more. Only when they wintered in Rome or came to London did Robert, at Elizabeth's urgings, regularly attend society functions. Those who met them together invariably remember her silent though friendly nature and his talkative geniality. A letter from Thomas Chase to his family in America denotes these traits. Written from Italy on 15 June 1854 while his visit with the Brownings was still fresh in his mind, it gives us an intimate glimpse into their lives:

> I requested an interview with the Brownings in a note in which I alluded to my having gathered flowers for Mrs. B. in Greece. I received immediately a very kind reply in which they gave me a very cordial invitation to call, and appointed half past ten the next morning as the hour. (Now what I may have to say of them, I must have it understood beforehand that not one word is to be printed or in any way made public. . . .) I found Mrs. Browning seated in an armchair, her dark complexioned face, & the lines under her eyes, marked with traces of suffering, but with it the stamp of a high intellect and exquisite sensibility. Her forehead was shaded with thick black curls. She is short, slight, very slight and weak, & has some slight appearance of deformity about the chest. Her dress, black silk I think on the bust, & a skirt with white spots. Her voice is low & tremulous, & very feeble, but sensitive & *expressive*. She thanked me very kindly for the pleasure the flowers had given her, & showed me the book in which they had been most tastefully arranged . . . Mr. Browning entered in a few minutes; a fine healthy-looking man of some five and thirty . . . with black hair very abundant, a sprinkling of gray in his beard, a rather dark complexion, and most expressive blue eyes. He talked with the greatest fluency in simple, natural, strong English: he is a great talker. Mrs. Browning said little, but what she did say had meaning and came just at the right time. . . . Both Mr. & Mrs. Browning are very *democratical* in their opinions. Mrs. Browning said, 'that it's the great thing, for a people to be *democratic*, no matter what their form of government, whether republican or monarchical.' . . . Browning says his constitution has undergone an entire change since his marriage & residence in Tuscany, what with the change of climate & diet. He used to have dizzy headaches. His circulation is slow, & a Physician told him he ought to live 100 years. Mrs. B's circulation is too rapid. . . . I left, amidst kind expressions of regret that I had not sought them sooner, and invitations to call again.[12]

After Elizabeth's death and as Browning's literary reputation grew, he became part of the London literary and social scene. In this period when he was dining out approximately five times a week, meeting Mr. Browning was not too difficult an achievement. From the last twenty-five years of his life hundreds of carte-de-visite photographs survive showing the respectable, prosperous poet, with neatly trimmed white beard—a sixty- and a seventy-year-old public man. It is from this period, too, that most accounts of meeting Mr. Browning survive. As the numbers increase, so their importance decreases, until after 1870 the man himself is hidden behind a smoke screen of trivia. Indeed, there is every reason to suggest that Browning encouraged this protective smoke screen which biographers have found so difficult to clear.

Meeting Robert Browning in the last twenty-five years of his life at home in Warwick Crescent or De Vere Gardens meant experiencing a routine which varied only slightly from guest to guest. The ingredients of the conversation would include talk about his son's latest painting or sculpture; reference to Elizabeth would lead naturally to a visit to the study to look at specially selected books with her delicately written annotations, followed by rather bland statements about what a wonderful person she had been. Dinner conversation, at home and abroad, would be anecdotal—with Browning frequently at the centre of the table, vividly relating some story from his wide reading or about public figures. He was always interested in his fellow guests and was so courteous and friendly that many who met him felt that he had been speaking to them alone. A number of his female friends mistook this affectionate concern and lively conversation for something deeper, only to have their expectations disappointed.

It is easy to see this public Browning as the poet in comfortable middle age enjoying the adulation of friends, acquaintances and the Browning Society. However, Browning seldom spoke about events of his past life; although he occasionally refought old literary battles at dinner, he was no gossip. His table-talk was an art rather than a confession. Indeed, his bonhomie enabled him to distance himself from friends and acquaintances. The same is true of his later letters. Friends were placed in categories, according to their interests, and Browning's letters to each, affectionate though they often are, are highly selective in what they tell, and in many cases add up to very little. Browning's public *persona* was as vivid as any he invented to speak his poems. Just occasionally the façade cracked, as in his outburst against Edward FitzGerald which reached the pages of *The Athenæum* in 1889—after Browning learned of a derogatory remark that FitzGerald had once made about Elizabeth.

The need for this *persona* lies partly in the hostile reception of Browning's early poetry, which forced him on the defensive and led to twenty years of wounded pride and self-justification. Ever after, Browning was sensitive to any form of criticism. But this sensitivity was itself the product of his complex emotional and psychological makeup. Throughout his life, Browning, outwardly confident and assured, needed the security of an intimate in whom he could confide and on whom he could totally rely. At different periods of his life he found his security in three people: his mother, his wife and his sister Sarianna.[13] His relationship with each was simultaneously as protector and protected.

Robert Browning was far more difficult to get to know than was his wife. Elizabeth was prepared to share her feelings and thoughts with a close circle and to give something of herself to most of those she met, and we see this generous rich spirit in *Aurora Leigh*. Ostensibly the more extroverted, Browning assumed a defensive pose which towards the end almost became the man. With the speaker in "House" he declined to sonnet-sing about himself or his life:

> No: thanking the public, I must decline.
> A peep through my window, if folks prefer;
> But, please you, no foot over threshold of mine.

Most of those who met Robert Browning were lucky if they were even allowed a peep through the window.

It is probably easier for us in the late twentieth century to cross the threshold and meet both the Brownings than it was for those in the Victorian age. Without their physical presence, we have to rely on photographs and paintings to tell us what they looked like—and on a single poorly-recorded cylinder for the sound of Robert's voice—but we have the advantage of nearly a hundred years of scholarship. Pen's controversial publication of his parents' love letters in 1899 unlocked a door which successive biographers and editors have slowly pushed open. As we near the centennial of Robert Browning's death, critical studies and editions of works and correspondence continue unabated. With this help, future generations can look forward to meeting the Brownings and getting to know them with a greater understanding and clarity.

1. Henriette Corkran, *Celebrities and I* (London: Hutchinson, 1902), p. 31.
2. Julian Hawthorne, *Hawthorne and His Circle* (London: Harpers, 1903), p. 341.
3. Quoted in W. Hall Griffin and H.C. Minchin: *The Life of Robert Browning* (London: Methuen, 1910), p. 163, where it is accepted without comment.
4. Anne Ritchie, *Records of Tennyson, Ruskin and Browning* (London: Macmillan, 1896), p. 240.
5. *Ibid.*, pp. 241–242.
6. For a detailed discussion of both versions of the Field Talfourd drawing, see William S. Peterson, "'My Spiritual Face': A Newly Discovered Portrait of Mrs. Browning," *Browning Institute Studies*, Vol. 5 (1977), pp. 1–22.
7. *Ibid.*, p. 15.
8. Quoted in Ian Jack, "Browning on *Sordello* and *Men and Women*: unpublished letters to James T. Fields," *Huntington Library Quarterly* (Summer 1982), p. 197.
9. Philip Kelley and Ronald Hudson, *The Brownings' Correspondence*, Vol. 3 (Winfield, Kansas: Wedgestone Press, 1985), p. 331.
10. Quoted in M.C. Meredith, *Robert Browning* (London: Common Ground, 1964), p. 9.
11. Thomas Powell, *Pictures of the Living Authors of Britain* (London: Partridge and Oakley, 1851), pp. 139–140.
12. From the manuscript letter, Haverford College, Pennsylvania.
13. During the last twenty years of Browning's life it was Sarianna, his constant companion, who alone shared his complete confidence. It is surprising that no biographer has yet investigated the part Sarianna played. To consider her role as being simply in charge of Browning's household is, I think, too simple a view. Her influence, for better or for worse, was profound.

Colour Plates

PLATE 1

Above: EBB's childhood home—Hope End Mansion. Located near the Malvern Hills, the house was built by her father in Turkish style. Bedroom and sitting room for EBB were at top left.

Left: EBB's father had this silver thimble with Hope End Mansion design specially made for his wife. EBB received it after her mother's death.

(Catalogue numbers 1, 4a)

PLATE 2

Right: Young EBB's copy of *The Book of Common Prayer*, with her name stamped in gilt on cover. The family's religious preference is shown by alteration, on title-page, from "Church of England" to "Church *in* England." *Below:* Painting was among the talents of EBB's mother, as shown by this watercolour of her five eldest (of twelve) children. EBB holds Samuel. Others, from left: Edward, Henrietta, and Mary—who died at age three. (Catalogue numbers 4b, 2)

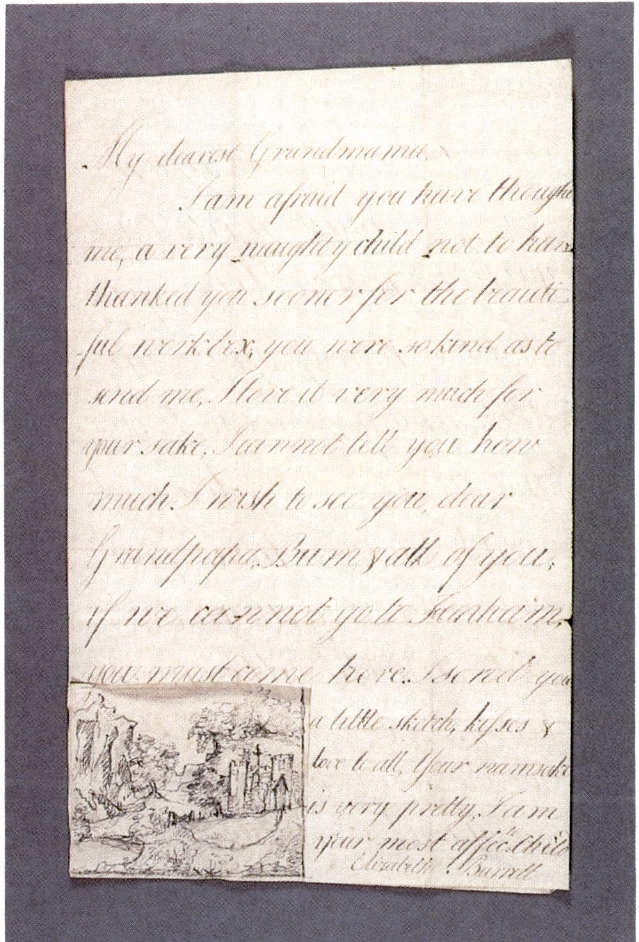

My dearest Grandmama,
I am afraid you have thought me, a very naughty child not to have thanked you sooner for the beautiful workbox, you were so kind as to send me, I love it very much for your sake, I cannot tell you how much I wish to see you, dear Grandpapa, Bummy & all of you, if we cannot go to Fenham, you must come here. I send you a little sketch, kisses & love to all, Your namesake is very pretty, I am your most affec. Child
Elizabeth Barrett

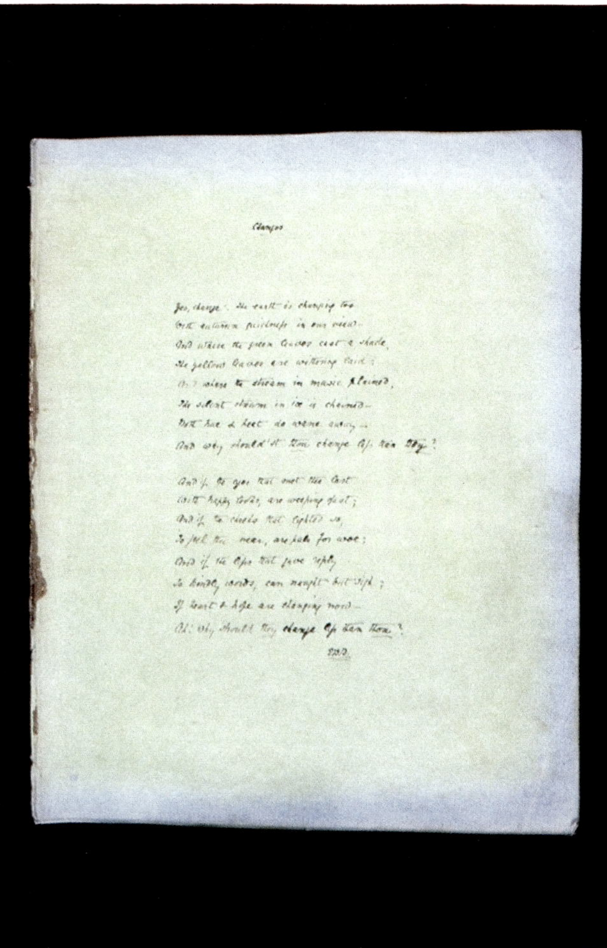

PLATE 3
Above: Ink sketch of a castle or possibly of Hope End. EBB's maternal grandmother sought to encourage her in needlework and sent a workbox. The child wrote a letter dutifully acknowledging the gift, with a sample of a type of work she preferred.
Above right: This early version of EBB's "Change upon Change," in her own hand, appears in an album she gave her sister Henrietta. The album is filled with mementoes of the Moulton-Barretts and their circle.
(Catalogue numbers 3, 6)

PLATE 4
The Barretts of Wimpole Street. EBB's brother Alfred, a talented amateur artist, painted these watercolour portraits of family members in 1843. *Above:* The last known likeness of EBB's father, Edward Moulton-Barrett.
Right: Portrait of EBB dated 27 September.
Opposite page: Five of EBB's sisters and brothers—Henrietta (upper left) and Arabella, Henry (center), Septimus (lower left) and Octavius.
(Catalogue numbers 10b, 11)

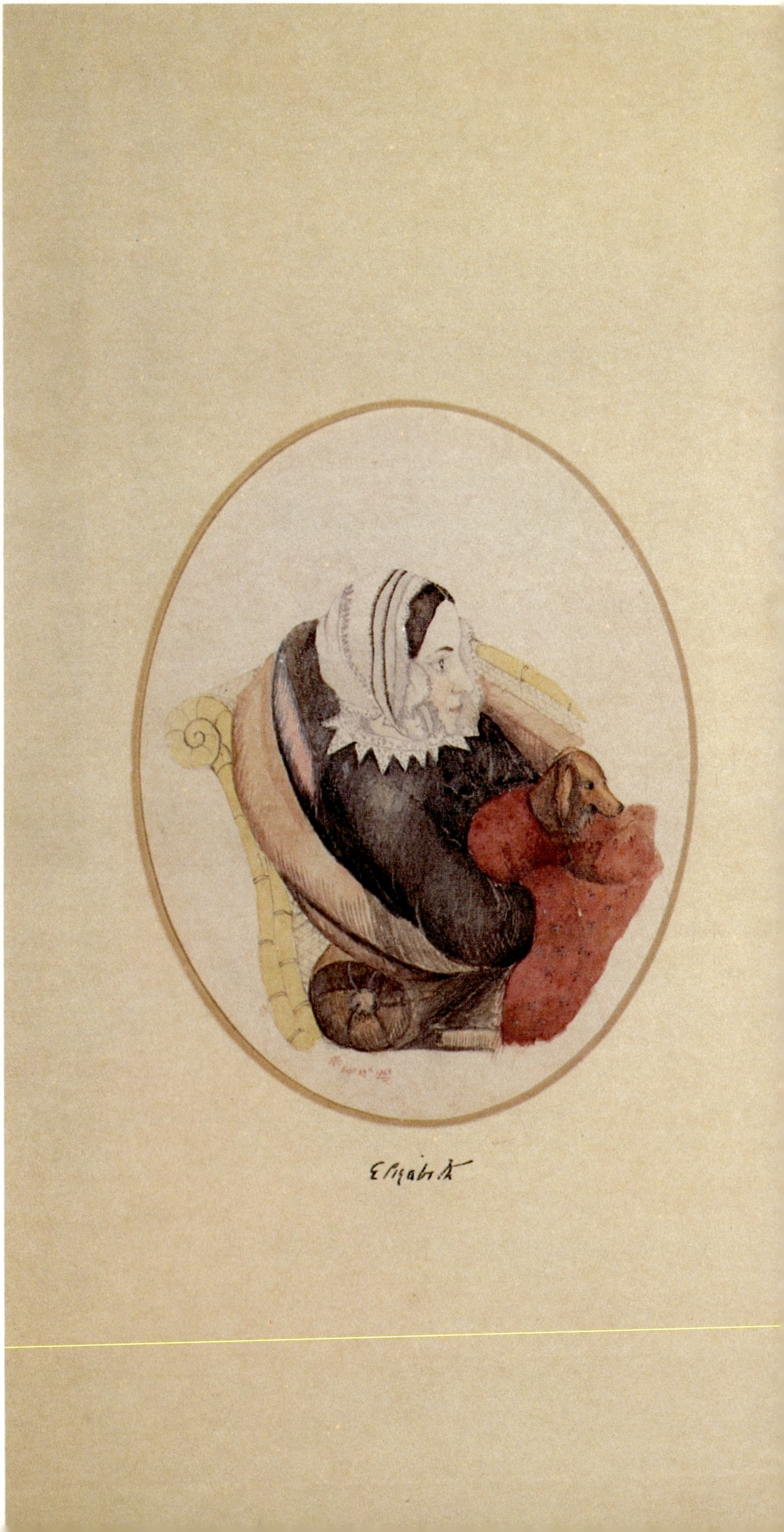

Henrietta
Aug - 3

Arabel

Henry
June 29 - 1843

Septimus
June 17 - 1843

Octavius

PLATE 5

Opposite page: Valentine from two Wimpole Street sisters to cousin Georgiana Elizabeth Barrett—poem by EBB, decorations by Arabella. The valentine with poem "What is under the rose" is accompanied by an envelope with 14 February 1844 postmark. At right is a portrait of Georgiana ("Lizzie") by Alfred Moulton-Barrett, who eventually married her.
Below: Rose is lifted to reveal the word "Love."
(Catalogue number 12)

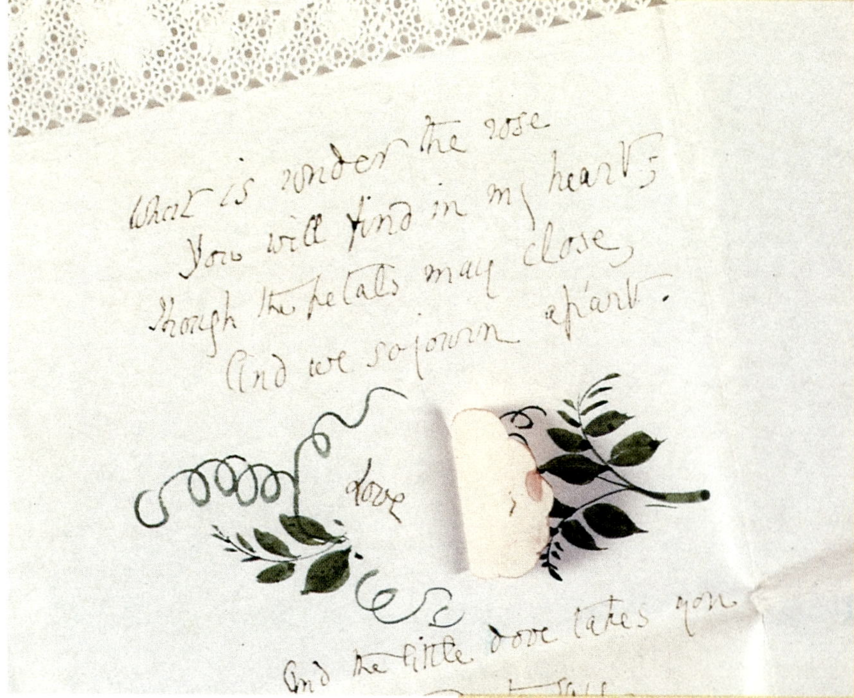

What is under the rose
You will find in my heart;
Though the petals may close,
And we sojourn apart.

Love

And the little dove takes you

PLATE 6
Right: Gown worn by RB at his christening, which took place at the York Street Independent Chapel, Walworth. RB mentioned the ceremony in a letter he wrote to EBB on 3 August 1845.
Below: This copy of *The Poetical Works of Dr. John Donne* belonged to RB, who made numerous annotations and eventually presented it to his friend Alfred Domett.
(Catalogue numbers 13, 18)

PLATE 7
Above: RB's sister, Sarianna, as painted in oil *circa* 1834 by unknown artist.
Right: Robert Browning, Sr., father of RB, as sketched in pencil *circa* 1864 by Sarianna.
(Catalogue numbers 16, 15)

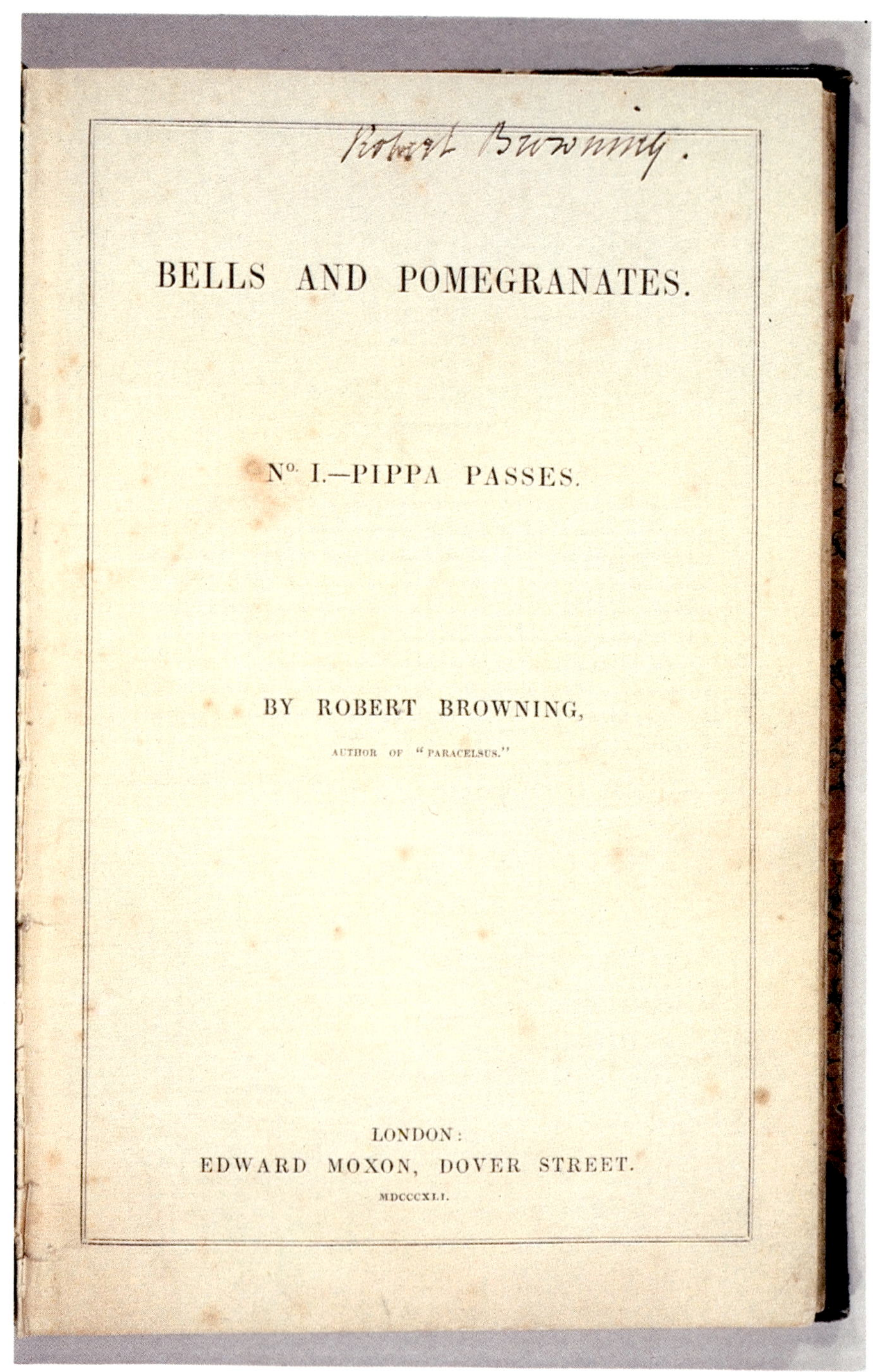

PLATE 8
RB's *Bells and Pomegranates*. This single volume containing all eight parts, owned and autographed by RB, is opened to No. I—"Pippa Passes." (Catalogue number 24)

PLATE 9
Oil painting done in the 1850's by Dante Gabriel Rossetti illustrates a line from "Pippa Passes": "'Hist!'—said Kate the Queen."
(Catalogue number 88a)

PLATE 10

Right: RB's writing portfolio, used in 1840's while he was producing *Bells and Pomegranates* and corresponding with EBB. Inside the front cover is a sketch by RB, with Greek and Hebrew lettering; also, inverted at upper left, is a quotation in his hand from EBB's "The Past."

Below: Front cover of writing portfolio.

(Catalogue number 26)

PLATE 11

Left: Silver inkstand used by EBB in the Wimpole Street home and previously. It shows clearly in a pencil sketch of her by an unknown artist, made, probably at Hope End, when she was about 19.

Below: During their courtship, EBB dared to send RB 56 pages of criticisms of his poetry. These are now interleafed in a bound copy of Nos. VII and VIII of *Bells and Pomegranates*. Here, the book is opened to "The Flower's Name" and EBB's critique.

(Catalogue numbers 28a, 27)

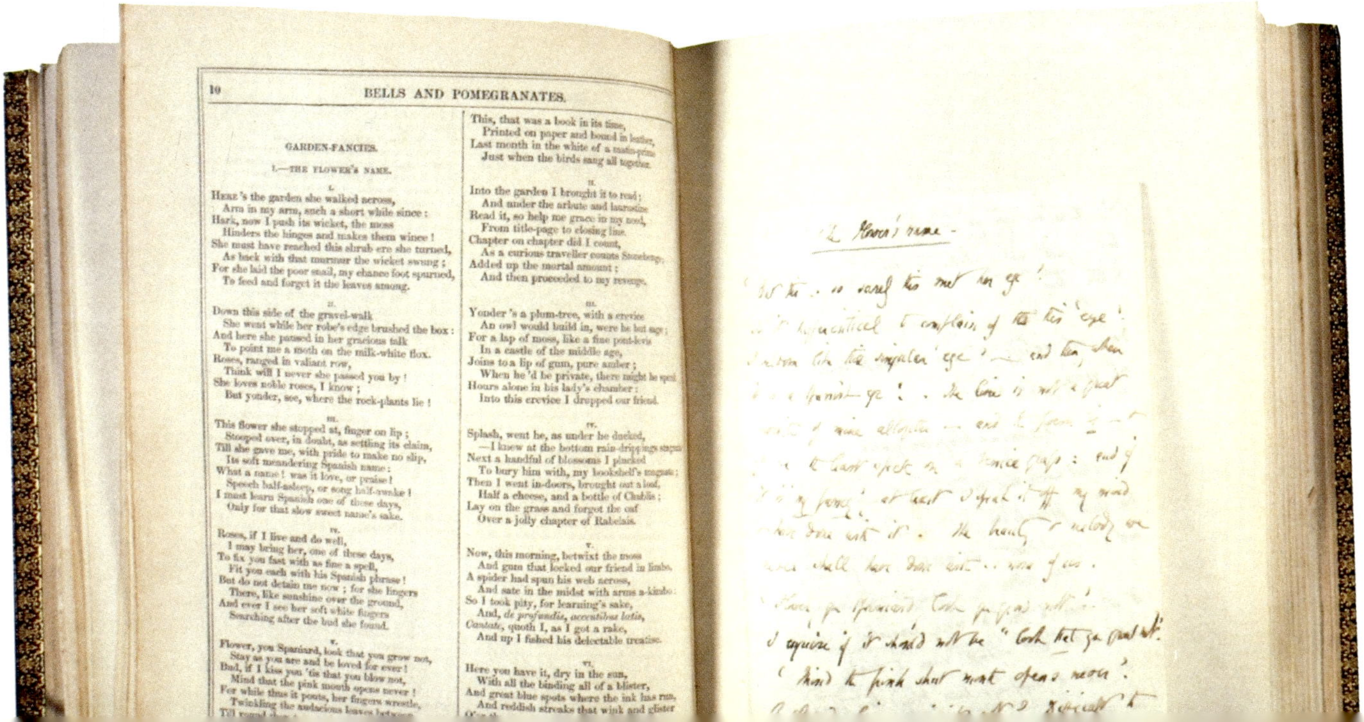

PLATE 12
The love letters of RB and EBB, written 1845–46, were kept in the containers pictured here.
Above: EBB used a collapsible morocco case for those she received.
Below: A marquetry box was RB's receptacle for letters from her.
(Catalogue numbers 28c, 28d)

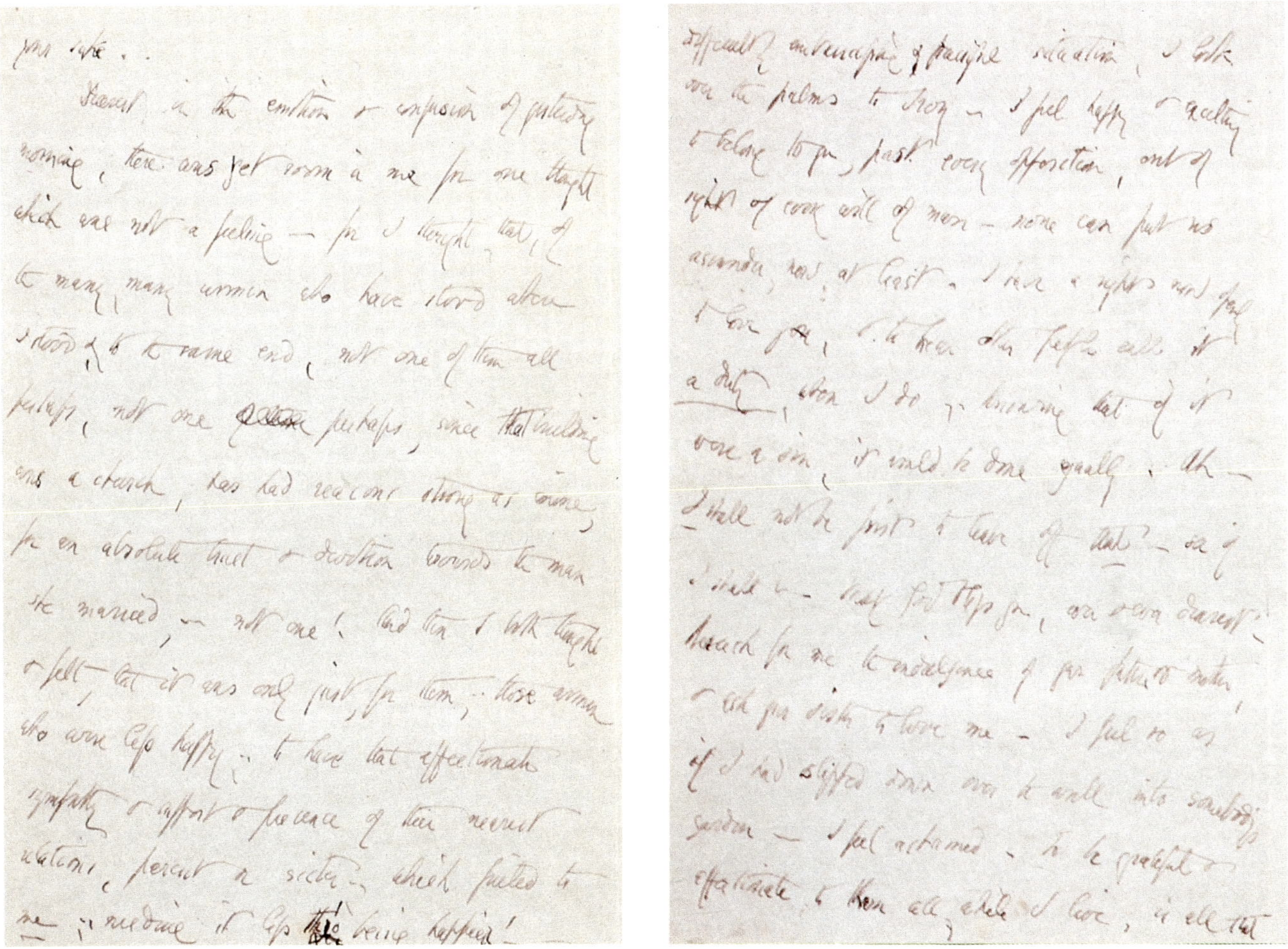

your sake . .

Except in the emotion & confusion of yesterday morning, there was yet room in me for one thought which was not a feeling — for I thought that, of the many, many women who have stood where I stood, & to the same end, not one of them all perhaps, not one perhaps, since that building was a church, has had reasons strong as mine, for an absolute trust & devotion towards the man she married, — not one! And then I both thought & felt, that it was only just, for them, .. those women who were less happy, .. to have that affectionate sympathy & support & presence of their nearest relations, parent or sister, .. which failed to me, .. needing it less through being happier!

difficult & embarrassing & painful situation, I look over the palms to Troy — I feel happy & exulting to belong to you, past every opposition, out of sight of every will of man — none can put us asunder, now, at least. I have a right now openly to love you, & to hear other people call it a duty, when I do, .. knowing that if it were a sin, it would be done equally. Ah — I shall not be first to leave off that — see if I shall! .. May God bless you, ever dearest. Beseech for me the indulgence of your father & mother, & ask your sister to love me — I feel so as if I had slipped down over the wall into somebody's garden — I feel ashamed — to be grateful & affectionate to them all, while I live, is all that

PLATE 13
RB and EBB communicated only by post during the time between their marriage and their leaving London. In this letter, written on the day after the wedding, EBB tells of her silent thoughts during the ceremony. (Catalogue number 28b)

PLATE 14

Right: Edwin, principal man-servant at the Barretts' Wimpole Street home, as sketched by EBB's brother Alfred on 13 September 1845. Note the elaborate livery.

Below: Button from Moulton-Barrett servant's livery, bearing family crests. Beside the button at left and right respectively are seen the crests of the Barrett and Moulton families in silver. (Catalogue number 25)

PLATE 15
American sculptor Harriet Hosmer, while with the Brownings in Rome in 1853, made a mould of their clasped hands. Of the many castings produced, most are in bronze. This is one of two known castings done in plaster. (Catalogue number 30)

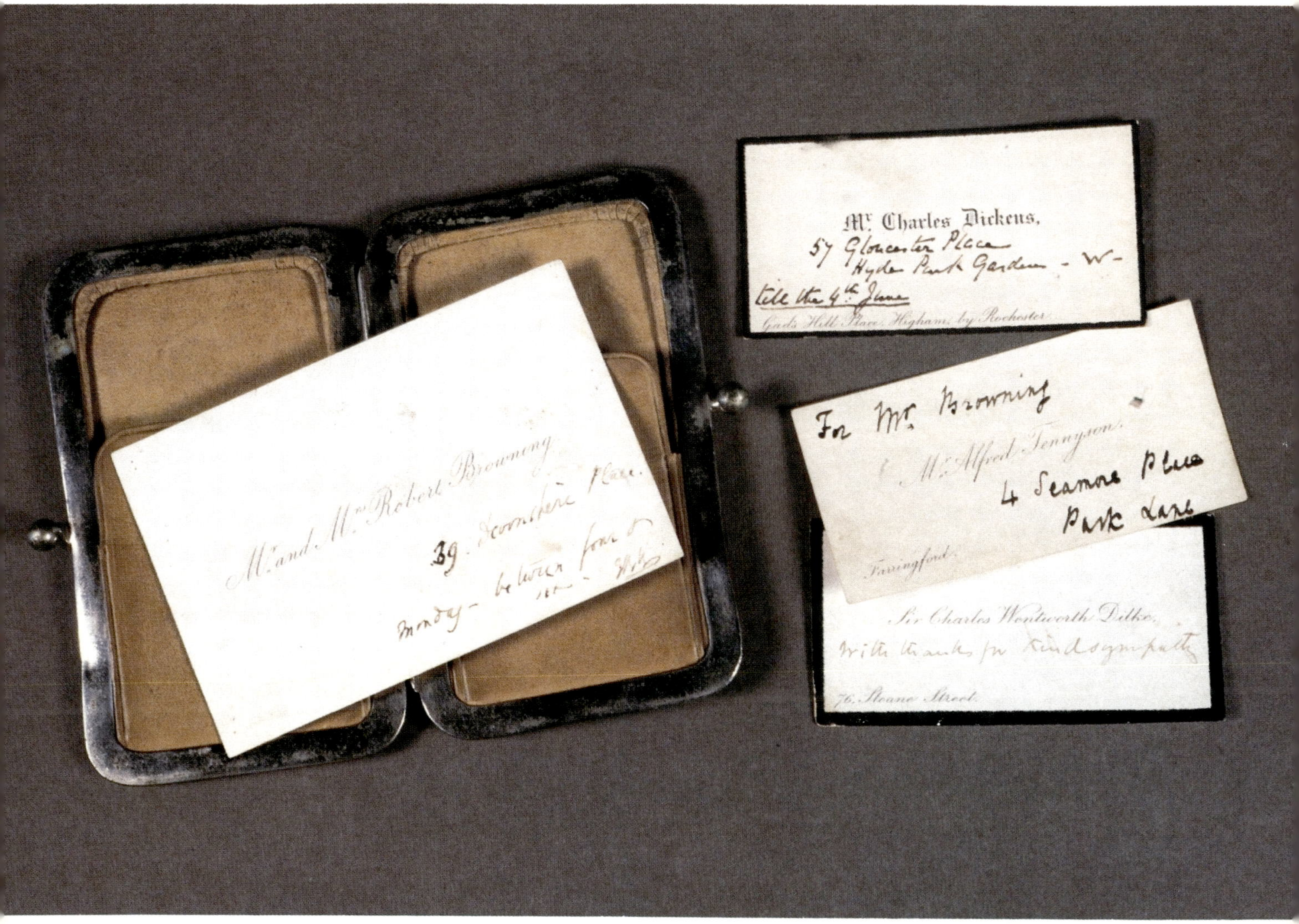

PLATE 16
Opposite page: Earliest known photograph of RB, made in Paris in 1856. It was discovered in New York City in August 1985.
Above: Calling cards with card case. At left is a card which EBB used in London in 1856. Also, cards left for the Brownings by prominent callers.
Right: Metal match box, a gift from Alfred Moulton-Barrett to RB.
(Catalogue numbers 33a, 48d, 48e, 72a)

PLATE 17

Above: Gold brooch with floral design and three amber topazes. The brooch was given by RB to EBB on their first wedding anniversary.

Above right: Honeymoon gift from RB to EBB, 1846. Cross and main components of chain are onyx; the cross is decorated with marcasite, silver, and central pearl.

Below right: Netted purse, EBB's wedding gift to RB.

Opposite page: Fair copy, in EBB's hand, of "How do I love thee?" sonnet in the *Sonnets from the Portuguese* sequence.

(Catalogue numbers 47a, 29b, 29a, 89a)

Sonnets from the Portuguese.

XLII

XLIII

How do I love thee? Let me count the ways –
I love thee to the depth and breadth and height
My soul can reach, when feeling out of sight
For the ends of Being and Ideal Grace.
I love thee to the level of everyday's
Most quiet need, by sun and candlelight.
I love thee freely, as men strive for Right;
I love thee purely, as they turn from Praise:
I love thee with the passion put to use
In my old griefs, and with my childhood's faith:
I love thee with the love I seemed to lose
With my lost saints, – I love thee with the breath,
Smiles, tears, of all my life! – and if God choose,
I shall but love thee better after death.

PLATE 18
Items from Casa Guidi.
Opposite page: Ornate tea caddy and silver teapot engraved with the initials "EBB."
Above: Berlin trembleuse cup and saucer, with floral design including the initial "B."
(Catalogue number 46)

PLATE 19

Above and left: Clothing accessories belonging to EBB. Lace mantilla and half-mittens, above. Silver Italian buttons displayed on ribbon, left. *Opposite page:* Chalk drawing of EBB, probably by Field Talfourd, after a portrait originally done by Talfourd in Rome in 1859.
(Catalogue numbers 47c, 47d, 47b, 36a)

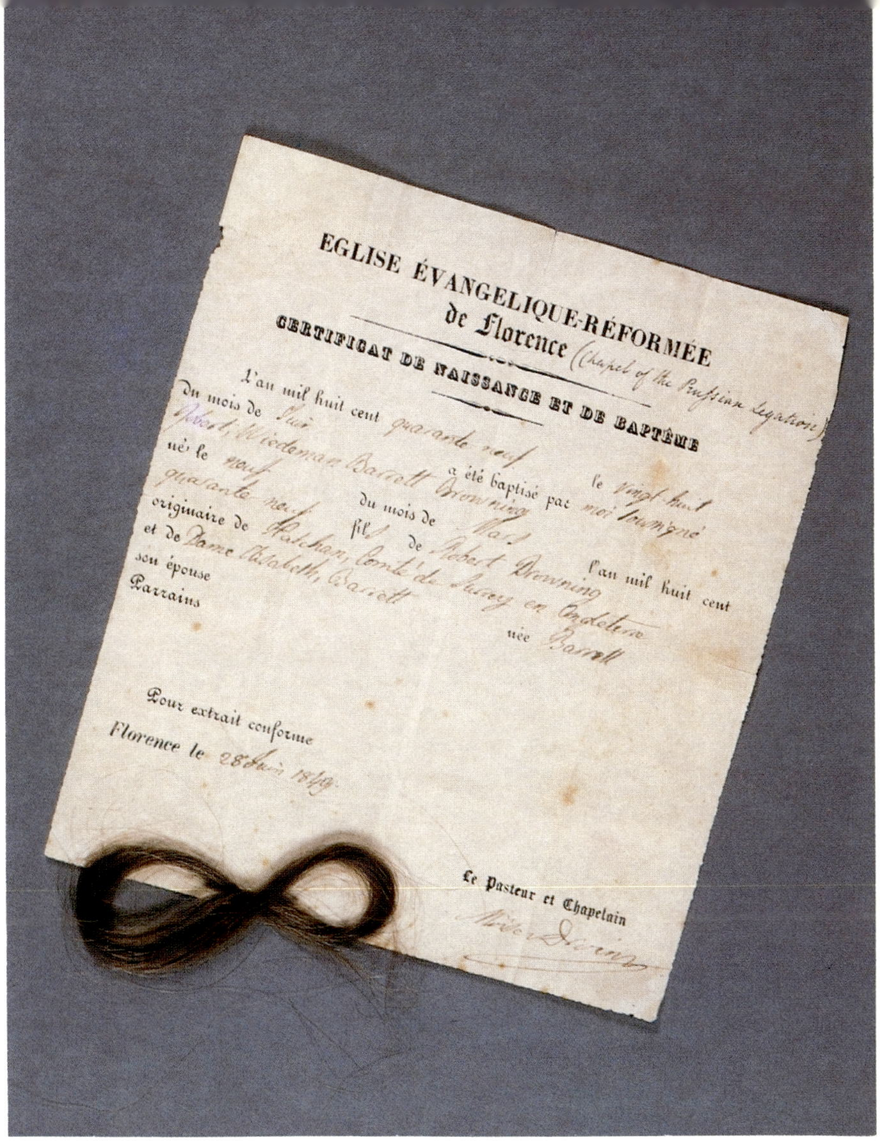

EGLISE ÉVANGELIQUE-RÉFORMÉE
de Florence (Chapel of the Prussian Legation)

CERTIFICAT DE NAISSANCE ET DE BAPTÊME

L'an mil huit cent quarante neuf le vingt huit du mois de Juin a été baptisé par moi soussigné Robert Wiedeman Barrett Browning né le neuf du mois de Mars l'an mil huit cent quarante neuf fils de Robert Browning originaire de Hatcham, Comté de Surrey en Angleterre et de Dame Elisabeth Barrett son épouse née Barrett

Parrains

Pour extrait conforme

Florence le 28 Juin 1849.

Le Pasteur et Chapelain

PLATE 20
Opposite page: Bust of Pen Browning by Alexander Munro; finished marble was exhibited at the Royal Academy in 1859.
Above left: Certificate of birth and baptism for Pen, born in 1849 in Florence. Lock of his hair, cut when he was one month old, was sent by EBB to her sister Henrietta.
Above right: An 1860 photograph of Pen from Alessandri Studios, Rome.
(Catalogue numbers 43, 41, 42)

PLATE 21
Above: The *Drawing Room at Casa Guidi* by George Mignaty. This oil painting was commissioned by RB shortly after EBB's death.
Opposite page: A mahogany folding chair with plush seat and back support (with carving detail). This chair may also be seen in the lower left corner of the Mignaty oil. In an 1882 portrait, RB is pictured in academic attire and seated in the folding chair.
(Catalogue numbers 50a, 51e, 65a)

1869. Rome.

PLATE 22
Opposite page: A folding fan (with handle detail). The fan is of dark green muslin with a gold border. It was used by EBB and bears her inscription. The fan may be seen on a folding deck arm chair in the Mignaty oil.
Left: A bronze taper stand used at Casa Guidi. The stand is seen in the Mignaty oil on one of two walnut tables.
Above: Tennyson Reading *Maud*. This black ink and sepia wash by Dante Gabriel Rossetti is dated 27 September 1855. The Rossetti wash may be seen to the left of the fireplace in the Mignaty oil. This work was later kept atop a bookcase in RB's study in De Vere Gardens, London.
(Catalogue numbers 51f, 51d, 120b)

PLATE 23
Opposite page: Madonna from the Italian School is an oil on canvas done *circa* 1500. It appears to the right of the screened bookcase in the Mignaty oil.
Above: An Italian escritoire with a folding top and drop front. The desk, fitted with 12 drawers, was used at Casa Guidi.
Right: One of two matching side chairs constructed of olive-wood with wicker bottoms. Both chairs were used at Casa Guidi and were presented by RB to the Edmund Tweedy family after EBB's death.
(Catalogue numbers 51b, 52)

PLATE 24
Upper left: Bronze plaque featuring head of Æschylus, seen at right of fireplace in the Mignaty oil.
Lower left: Two Children, Our Saviour and St. John, with a Lamb is a watercolour by Bartolomé Esteban Murillo.
Upper right: Portrait of Pen Browning at piano, by Euphrasia Fanny Haworth.
Lower right: Two Saints from the Sienese School, oil on single wood block, painted *circa* 14th century.
(Catalogue numbers 51c, 52c, 51a, 52d)

PLATE 25
Left: Tomb of EBB was designed by Frederic Leighton. James Martin, a family friend, received this photograph in 1867 from RB. Another photograph of the tomb was joined with a photograph of Hope End, EBB's childhood home, in a shield-shaped frame—kept by RB in his study.
Below: William Surtees Altham, EBB's brother-in-law, recorded her death in his diary. Four volumes are extant.
(Catalogue numbers 56, 55a)

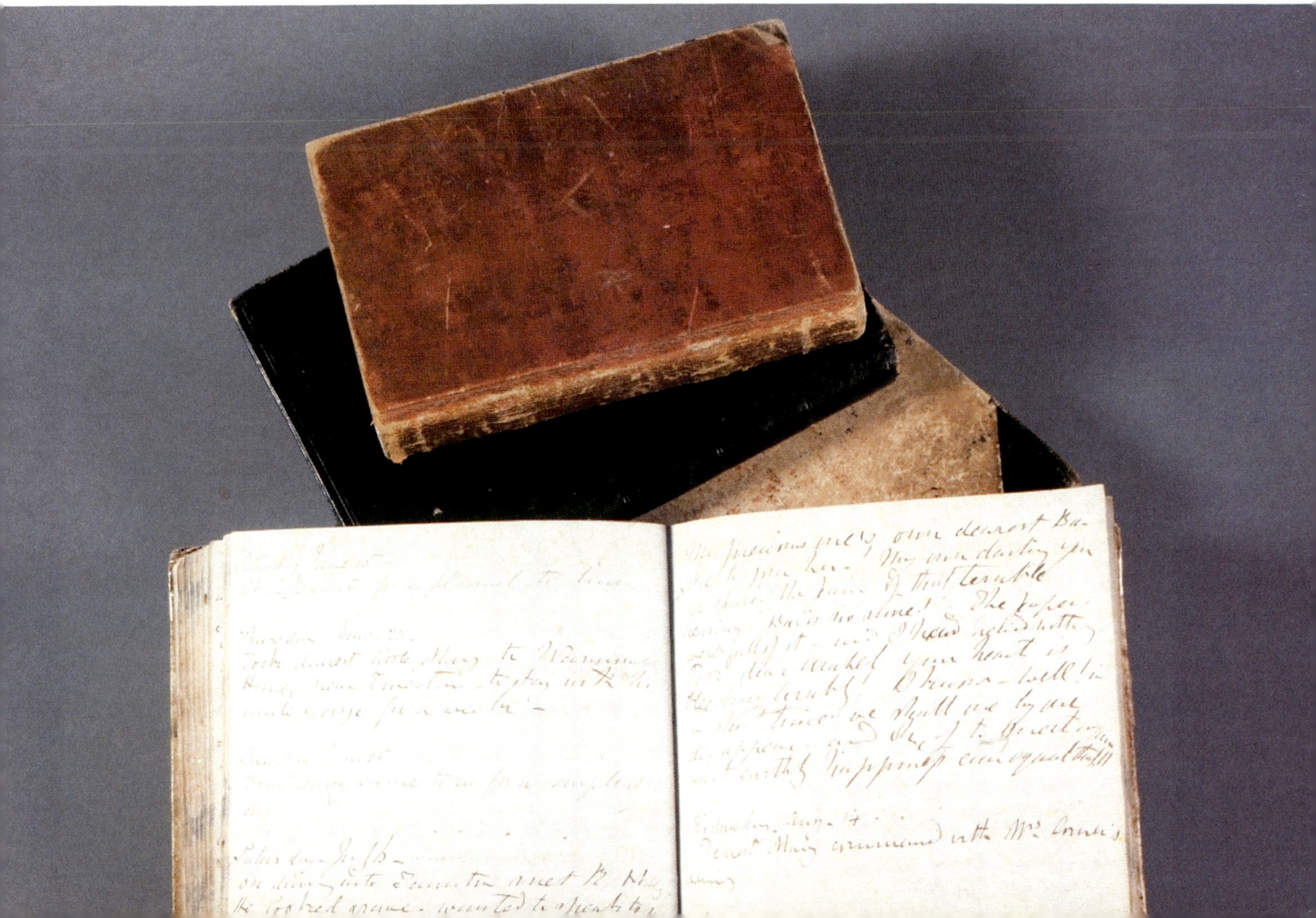

PLATE 26
Above: Commemorative plaque made of terra-cotta. This plaque was on the façade of 19 Warwick Crescent, London, and removed before the building was demolished in the 1960's. RB lived there from May 1862 until October 1887.
Above right: View from RB's study by Arthur Sanderson.
Right: Bust of Percy Bysshe Shelley by Marianne Hunt, owned by RB.
Extreme right: Signet finger ring bears intaglio of Browning crest and motto, a lion rampant upon a shield above *virtute*. The band of 22-carat gold is set with a green bloodstone. This ring, worn by RB for about 40 years, is visible in several of his portraits. (Catalogue numbers 58c, 58b, 83c, 48a)

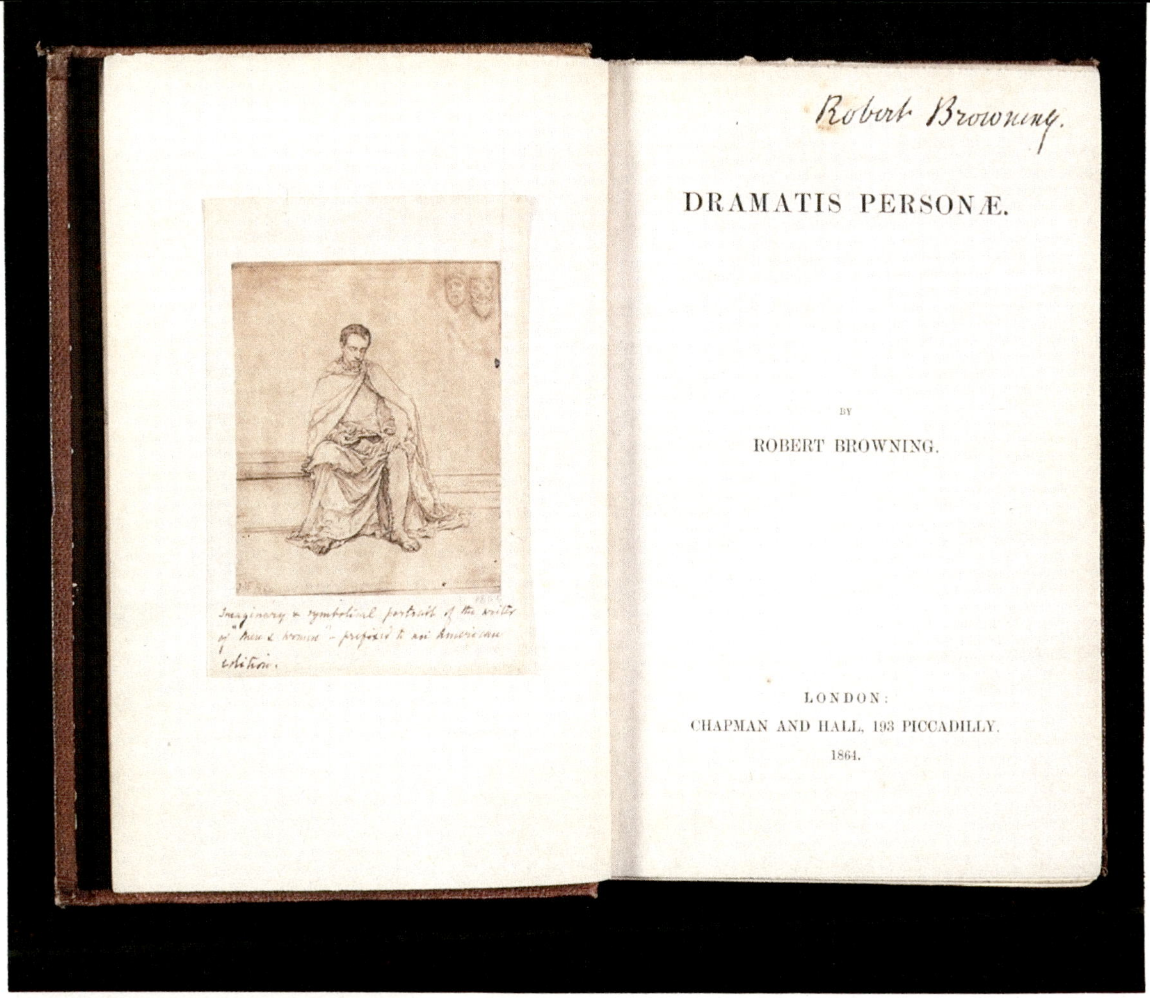

PLATE 27
Above: RB's *Dramatis Personae* was published in London in 1864. There are several manuscript corrections in this volume from RB's library, and an addition of three stanzas to "Gold Hair" done in his hand.
Left: Antique marble head was in the center of pieces ranged atop the bookcase in RB's study in De Vere Gardens, London. It may be seen in the watercolour of the study by Felix Moschelles, commissioned by Pen Browning upon his father's death. (Catalogue numbers 61, 60)

PLATE 28
Opposite page: Portrait of Joseph Antoine Milsand by Pen Browning, 1882. Milsand, an author and family friend, exchanged gifts with RB, Sr. and RB. An 1884 photograph depicts RB and Joseph Milsand looking at another painting by Pen Browning. RB was godfather to Milsand's grandson, Robert Blanc-Milsand.
Left: Bronze bust of Pompilia, the heroine of *The Ring and the Book*, was done in 1886 by Pen Browning. Because so many of his works were either lost or destroyed, it is difficult to assess Pen's talents.
(Catalogue numbers 70, 87e)

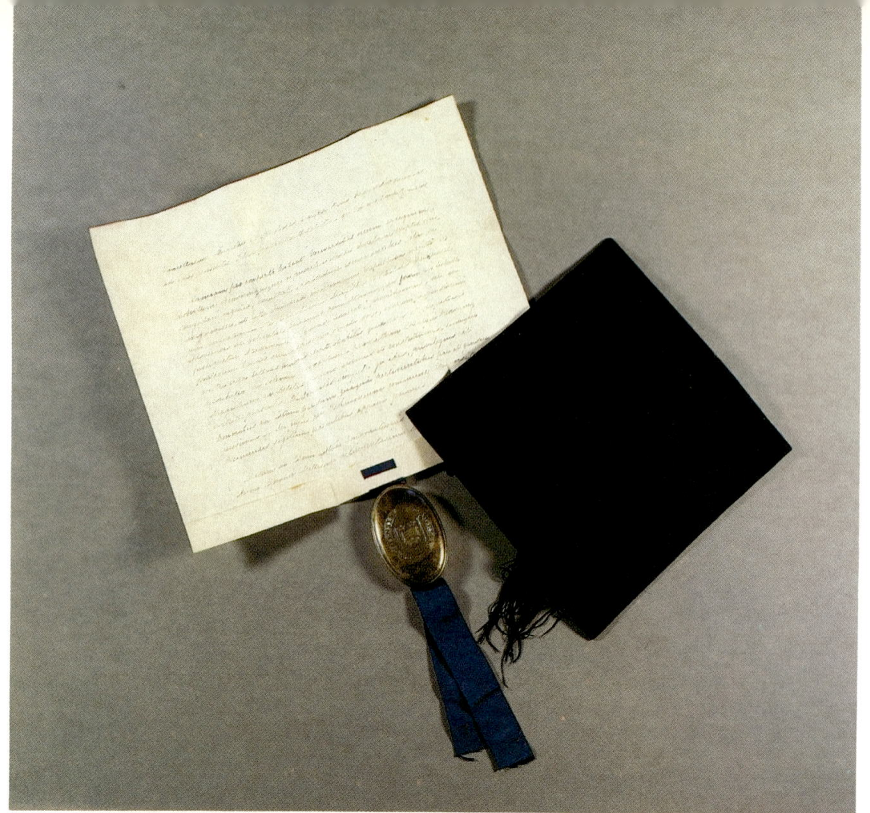

PLATE 29

Above: Diploma and mortarboard. The diploma was granted to RB by Oxford University and conferred upon him the degree of M.A. in 1867. The mortarboard belonged to RB along with the academic robe seen in Plate 21.

Below: Procession of Dons, Balliol College, is inscribed "June 30, '86, Balliol, Oxford. RB."

Opposite page: Personal effects owned by RB. Those pictured are dressing case, gloves, collar tie and cravat, and silver paper knife.

(Catalogue numbers 64, 65b, 66, 72)

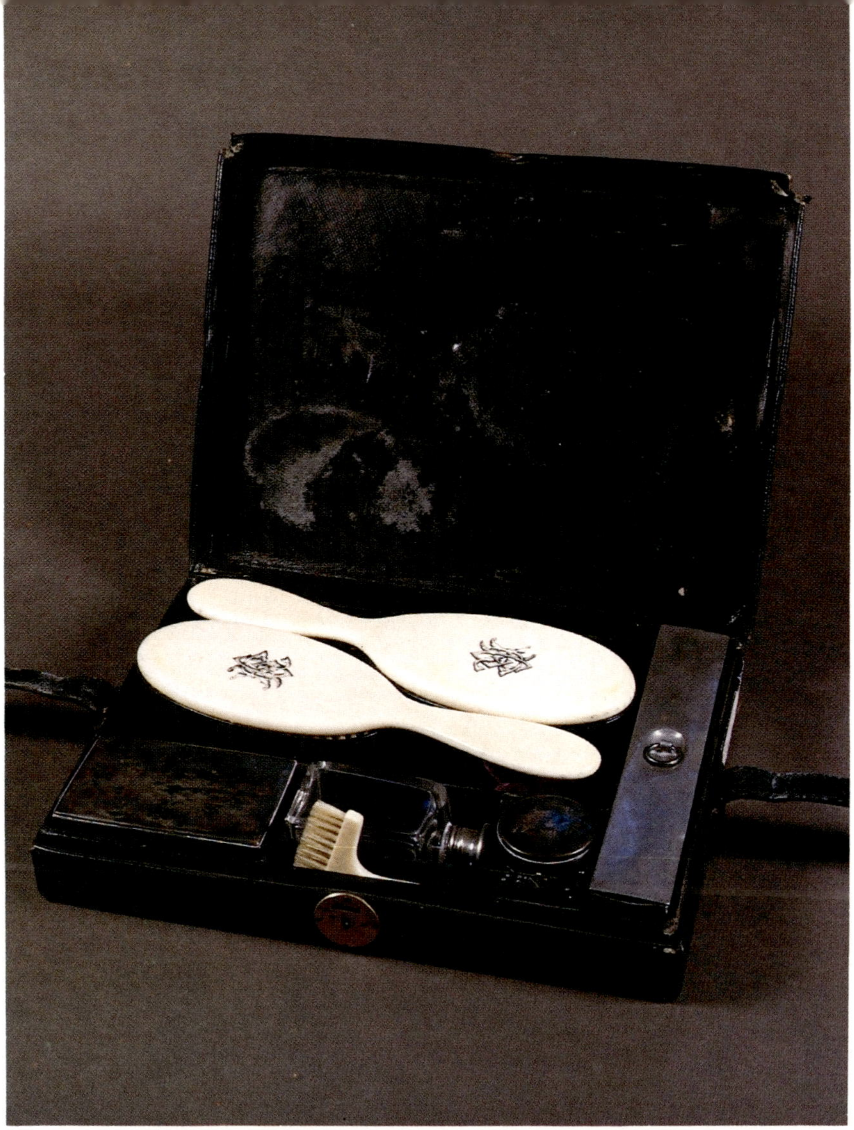

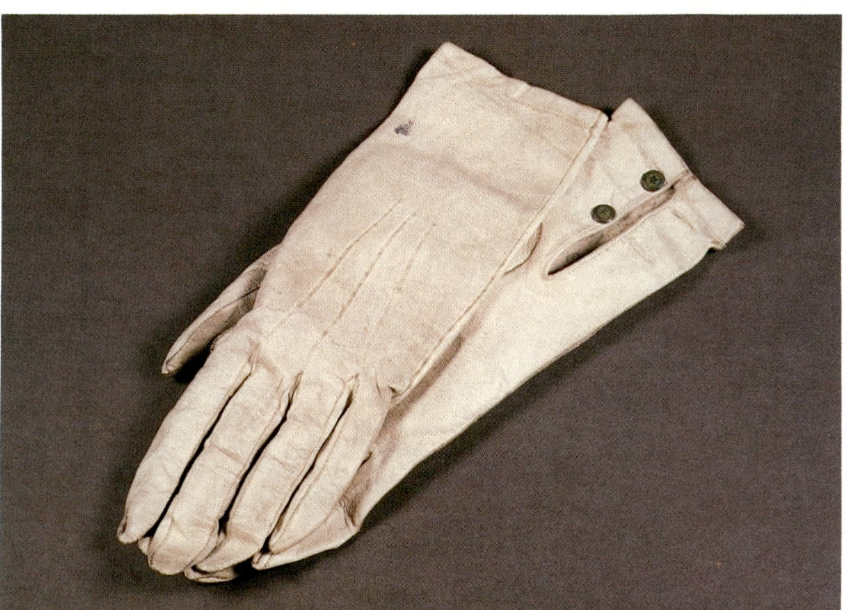

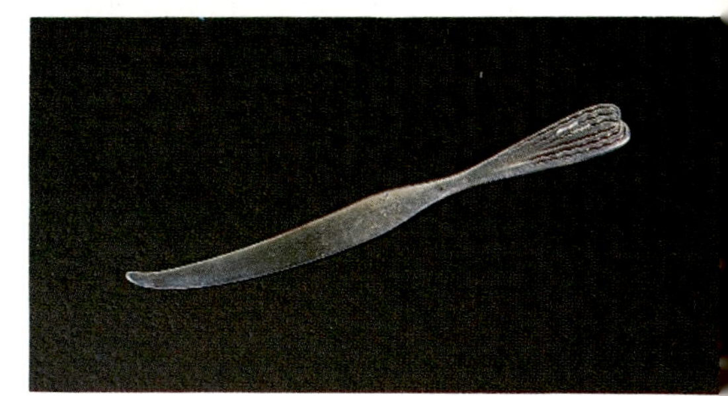

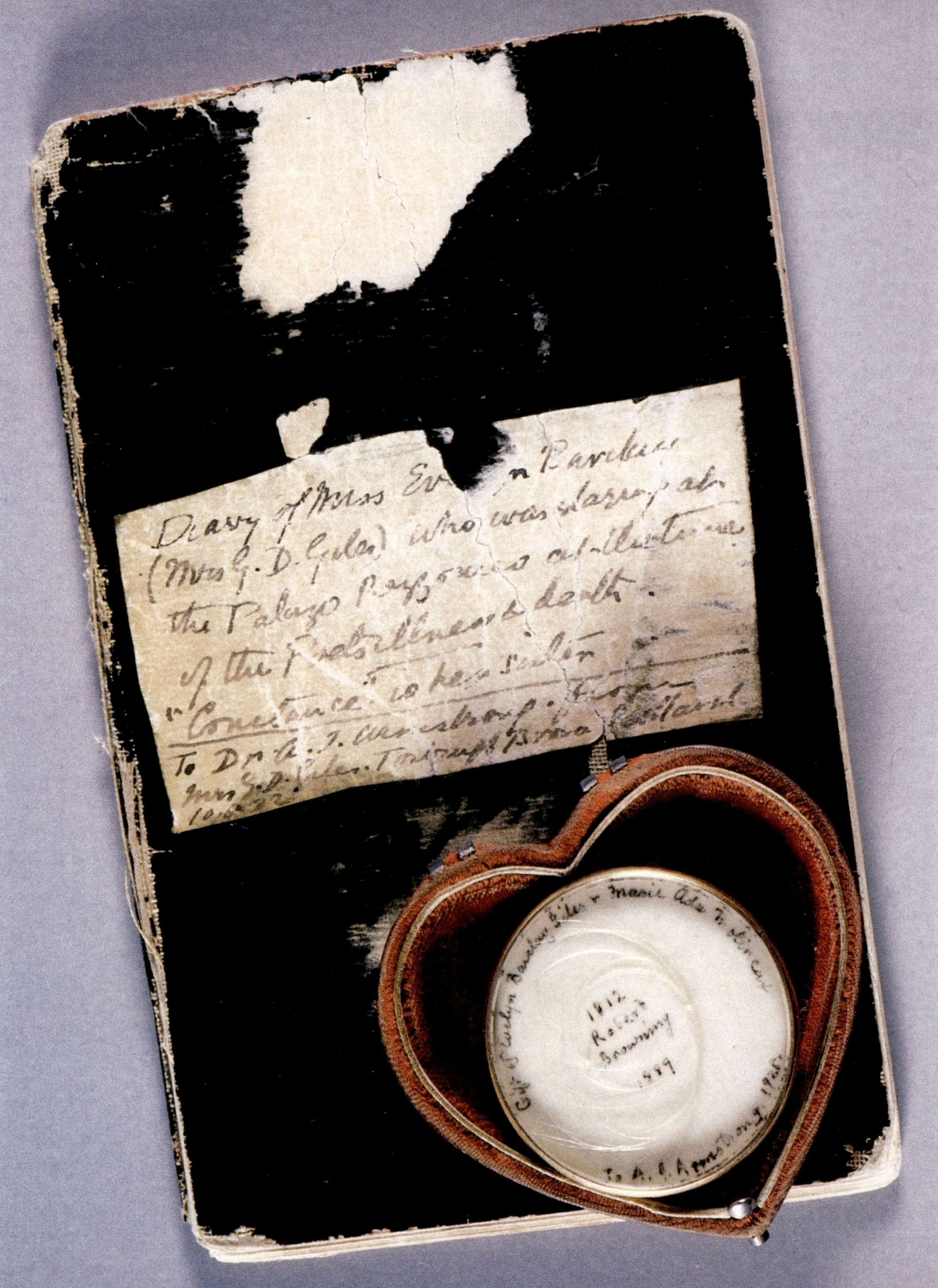
1812
Robert
Browning
1889

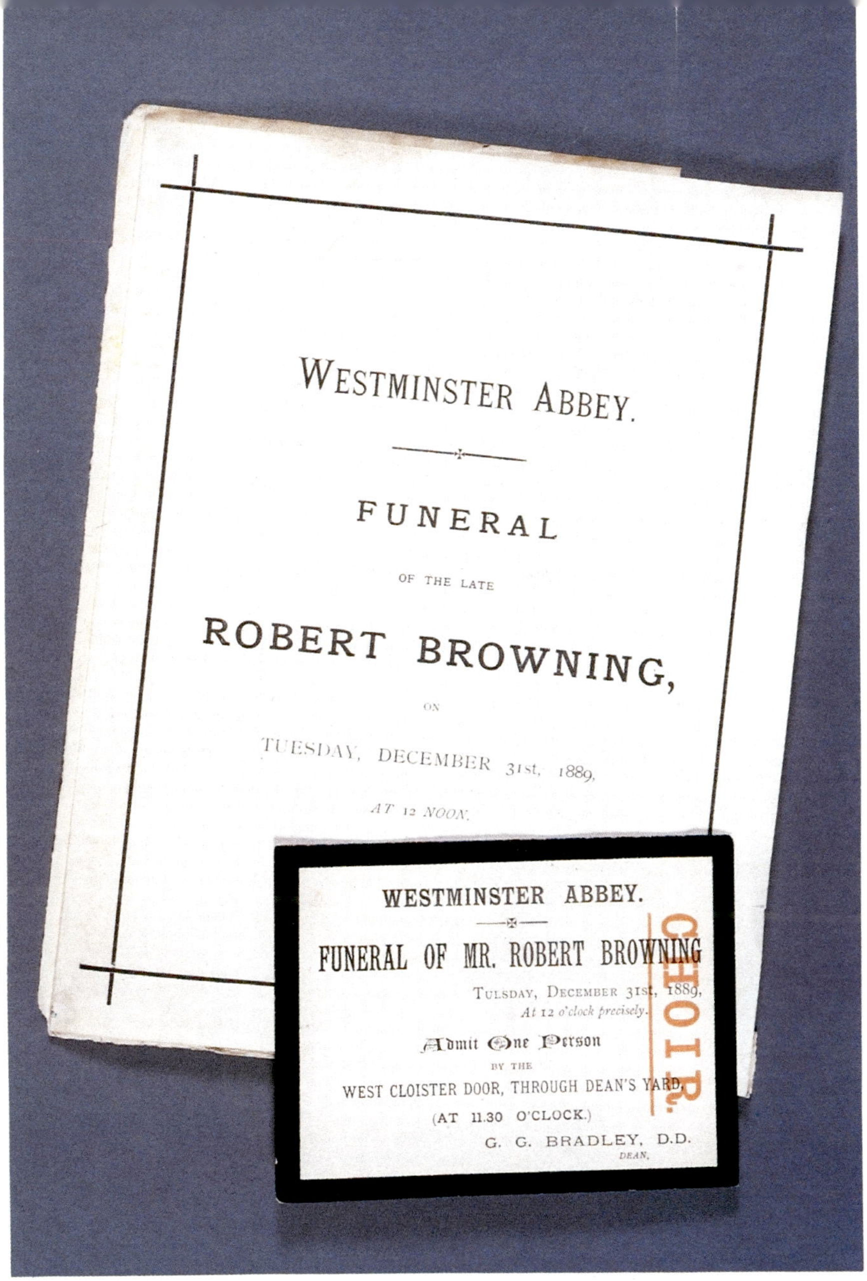

WESTMINSTER ABBEY.

FUNERAL

OF THE LATE

ROBERT BROWNING,

ON

TUESDAY, DECEMBER 31st, 1889,

AT 12 NOON.

WESTMINSTER ABBEY.

FUNERAL OF MR. ROBERT BROWNING

TUESDAY, DECEMBER 31st, 1889,
At 12 o'clock precisely.

Admit One Person

BY THE

WEST CLOISTER DOOR, THROUGH DEAN'S YARD,

(AT 11.30 O'CLOCK.)

G. G. BRADLEY, D.D.
DEAN.

CHOIR.

PLATE 30
Opposite page: Evelyn Barclay's diary provides an account of RB's last days and death, 12 December 1889 in Venice, Italy. On top of the diary is a locket, owned by Evelyn Barclay, containing a lock of the poet's hair, cut by Fannie Browning and given to Evelyn Barclay some time after RB's death.
Left and lower left: Items from RB's London funeral 31 December 1889. These are the funeral program, casket leaves, and a white silk ribbon from the casket.
(Catalogue numbers 78, 79b, 80)

The Catalogue

MEETING THE BROWNINGS

THIS EXHIBITION aims to tell an old tale in a new way. The familiar story of the romance between Robert and Elizabeth Barrett Browning, known through novel, play, musical and television drama, is here recreated by means of original books, letters, manuscripts and possessions of the two participants and their families. It is hoped that this arrangement of original material will have sufficient impact to fulfil the exhibition's main aim which, quite simply, is to enable visitors to meet the Brownings.

The exhibition is in three closely-linked parts. The first is biographical and outlines the story of the Brownings' lives with only slight reference to their writing. Portraits and photographs are used to show the likenesses of Robert and Elizabeth at different ages, and numerous everyday objects which they owned are displayed. These have been quite deliberately chosen to emphasize the ordinariness of their lives and to dispel the air of unreality which so often surrounds their story.

Starting with the early life and work of both poets, this section moves through the dramatic events at Wimpole Street to the couple's happy married life at Casa Guidi in Florence. An attempt has been made through the use of surviving furniture and paintings to give an impression of what the Brownings' surroundings were like in Italy, when they were creating such works as *Aurora Leigh* and *Men and Women*. The items on display reflect Robert's move back to England on the death of Elizabeth and his eventual public acceptance and recognition as a major poet.

The second section is concerned with their art. It makes no attempt to be comprehensive. Six works of Robert Browning and three of Elizabeth have been selected. While there is no substitute for reading the poems themselves, this display of first editions is intended to stimulate an interest in the works by showing something of the creative process which went into them.

The third section is wider-ranging. It traces the friendships of the Brownings with nineteen men and women, none of whom is a member of either family. These nineteen have been chosen to display the variety of the Brownings' friends; some are familiar names, others have been forgotten, while a few never left the domestic world where the Brownings met them. The nature of the friendships varies. There are close personal friends of long standing, as well as business acquaintances, teachers and travelling companions. Each, however, plays a part in the Browning story. Taken together, they make up a representative cross-section of the age in which the Brownings lived and the circle in which they moved.

One of the criteria used in selecting the nineteen friends was that each should be sufficiently known to the Brownings to be given a presentation copy of at least one of their volumes of poetry. Thus, friends and art are linked. The arrangement of this third section, from friends of early youth to those of old age, reinforces the biographical approach of the first section. In this way the exhibition is as complete as one could realistically expect. It is our hope that all who visit the exhibition will discover something new, something interesting, about the Brownings, whether they are meeting them for the first time or renewing old acquaintance.

Their Lives

Elizabeth Barrett Barrett's Early Years

1. Hope End Mansion: View from the Lower Pond
Watercolour by A.G. Turley, date unknown

In 1809 when EBB was three years old, her father purchased the 475-acre estate of Hope End between Ledbury and Malvern. During the next six years he built a large house decorated with minarets and domes in the contemporary oriental style. The building, which incorporated some of the original Queen Anne house, was influenced by the Repton designs for the Royal Pavilion at Brighton, and reminded Mary Moulton-Barrett of scenes from the *Arabian Nights*. Here EBB and her brothers and sisters grew up enjoying the ease and comfort of their well-appointed home and the excitements provided by the beautiful grounds, which had been landscaped by J.C. Loudon to include grottoes, a cascade, a deer park and a lake. The watercolour shows Hope End as it must have looked in 1830 when all Edward Moulton-Barrett's improvements were complete. Part of the old Queen Anne house, adapted as a brewhouse, stables and a laundry, can be seen at the rear to the right. The Moulton-Barretts were forced to leave Hope End in 1832 and the house was demolished in 1873. (Plate 1)

2. Elizabeth, her brothers and sisters
Watercolour and pencil by Mary Moulton-Barrett, June 1813

This watercolour, showing her five eldest children, was painted by EBB's mother at Hope End during the building of the new house. EBB (Ba), aged seven, is holding Samuel; Edward (Bro) is riding the dog; Henrietta has the cup, while little Mary is on her knees playing with building blocks.

The picture conveys well their happy childhood among the Malvern Hills. Another seven children were yet to be born to Mary and Edward Moulton-Barrett. Young Mary died in infancy, but the remaining eleven children all reached adulthood. (Plate 2)

3. Pencil Sketch by EBB
Included in a letter to Arabella Graham-Clark, 3 March 1814

EBB sent this sketch to her maternal grandmother with a letter thanking her for an early eighth birthday present. It is probably a romanticised picture of Hope End and shows the front of the house in its final form, overhung by the crags and trees of gothic fiction. (Plate 3)

4a. Thimble

b. *The Book of Common Prayer*, London, 1813

EBB's silver thimble and her prayer-book give an insight into life at Hope End. The thimble, with Hope End in bas-relief, was specially made for EBB's mother and demonstrates the pride Edward Moulton-Barrett clearly had in his new property. (After her mother's death, EBB was given this memento.) EBB's prayer-book has her name stamped in gilt on the decorated leather binding. The title page has been amended in ink to show the allegiance of the Moulton-Barretts to the nonconformist church rather than to the Church of England. Sermons were sometimes preached to the family on Sundays by the local minister, Revd. G.H. Curzon, in the schoolhouse-cum-chapel at the south gate of the main drive, as well as in Ledbury Baptist Church. (Plates 1 and 2)

5. Barrett, E.B., *The Battle of Marathon, A Poem*, London, 1820

EBB's first printed work, written when she was eleven and twelve, privately issued on or near her fourteenth birthday in an edition of fifty copies. This "great epic" was inspired by her reading of Pope's translation of Homer and, like its model, is written in heroic couplets. It is an ambitious work, four books long, an amazing achievement for a child. The poetry is merely pastiche, but an idea of its vigour and technical accomplishment can be obtained from its concluding lines:

> By vengeance fired, the Grecians from the deep
> With rage and shouting scale the lofty ship.
> Then in the briny bosom of the main
> They hurl in heaps the living and the slain;
> Thro' the wide shores resound triumphant cries,
> Fill all the seas, and thunder thro' the skies.

6. Barrett, E.B., "Changes," autograph ms., ca. 1831

The album in which this rough draft of an early poem appears was given by EBB to her sister Henrietta in 1831 and was used as a scrapbook until Henrietta's death. The poem, in EBB's hand, is an early version of her "Change upon Change," which appeared in a much altered form in *Blackwood's Edinburgh Magazine* in 1846, where it showed the clear influence of EBB's reading of Tennyson. On the verso of this page, EBB has made a copy of Revd. G.H. Curzon's poetical response to "Changes." In a similar fashion, EBB's brothers and sisters often made copies of *her* poems—for themselves and for friends. (Plate 3)

7. Photograph of 50 Wimpole Street

Edward Moulton-Barrett was forced to leave Hope End with his family in 1832 following the loss of part of his West Indian fortune. Several years in rented accommodations in Sidmouth and London followed, with most of the Moulton-Barrett furniture and books being kept in storage at Ledbury. In April 1838 the family moved to a permanent home at 50 Wimpole Street and started a new life surrounded by their own possessions. At first EBB was apprehensive, on account "of the gloominess of that street whose walls look so much like Newgate's turned inside out," but the house remained her home until her elopment in 1846. Edward Moulton-Barrett lived there until his death in 1857 and the house was pulled down in 1912.

Catalogue number 10a

8. View of Torquay
Letter from Edward Moulton-Barrett (Bro) to his brother Charles, 1 [*sic*, for 2] October 1839

In late 1838 EBB, suffering from a broken blood vessel in a lung, went to Torquay to enjoy the milder climate under the care of noted physician R.F. de B. Barry. She was accompanied by her eldest brother, Bro, who stayed with her during the next two years. This letter, headed with a vignette of Torquay Bay, was written by Bro to his brother Charles (Stormie) back in Wimpole Street, and shows, by means of arrows, the move he and EBB made from No. 3 to No. 1 Beacon Terrace on 1 October 1839. Bro refers to EBB's "state of deep affliction" over Dr. Barry's death "about 2 hours since." Ten months later Bro himself was dead, having drowned when his sailing boat capsized in Babbacombe Bay.

9. Barrett, E.B., *The Seraphim and other Poems*, London, 1838

"*The Seraphim* has faults enough—and weaknesses, besides—but my voice is in it, in its individual tones, and not inarticulately." EBB's assessment of her first important book is just. With this volume she established herself as a poet. Published in May before she left for Torquay in September, it attracted the kindly attention of Wordsworth and Landor. This presentation copy is particularly poignant. Dr. William Scully replaced Dr. Barry as EBB's physician at Torquay, and was responsible for looking after her during her collapse following Bro's death. As she left for London in her invalid carriage in September 1841, she gave "kind, *honest* Dr. Scully" this copy of *The Seraphim* as a memento.

10. Three Sketches of EBB
Drawings and watercolours by her brother Alfred, 1843

These three sketches vividly capture EBB's long years as an invalid in Wimpole Street. Drawn by her brother Alfred (Daisy), they all show Elizabeth lying on a sofa, well wrapped up with a rug, with Flush on her lap. She wears a bonnet which further protects her from draughts. The three form a series, for which the scenario might be as follows:

a. Unfinished pencil sketch heightened in watercolour, dated 12 July 1843. This drawing was taken from life.

b. Watercolour. A more finished version of (a) and copied from it on 27 September 1843. Alfred was painting several of his brothers and sisters at the time and clearly spent considerable pains over this version. (Plate 4)

c. Pencil sketch. This is another copy of (a), drawn on 12 December 1843, presumably for a member of the family who admired (b). More elaborate and fanciful in its setting, it shows through the window a summer scene in an idealized back garden of Wimpole Street.

11a. Edward Moulton-Barrett

b. Five of his children
Watercolours by Alfred Moulton-Barrett, 1843

Painted in the same year as the preceding sketches of Elizabeth, this watercolour of EBB's father is the only portrait of him known to survive from the 1840's. He is shown less as the tyrant depicted on stage and screen and more as the father "kind and tenderly attached to his children," as his son George remembered him. The five children—Arabella, Henrietta, Henry, Septimus and Octavius—were painted between June and August 1843. The father's likeness is dated September of the same year. (Plate 4)

The family's name, Moulton-Barrett, is a source of some confusion, since the "Moulton" was seldom used except in legal documents such as EBB's marriage certificate. Through Royal Licence and Authority in 1798, EBB's father was enabled to add his mother's maiden name "Barrett" to his own original surname "Moulton." This was done to perpetuate the Barrett line, since Edward and his brother Samuel (who likewise took the new name) were the only legitimate male heirs of their maternal grandfather, the wealthy and influential Edward Barrett of Cinnamon Hill, Jamaica. Later, EBB's father chose to emphasize "Barrett" still further by including it in the given names of all his children. Hence, EBB in early life called herself Elizabeth Barrett Barrett, then later replaced the second "Barrett" with "Browning."

Catalogue number 10c

12a. Lace Valentine

b. Lizzie Barrett
Watercolour by Alfred Moulton-Barrett, 1843

When they were young at Hope End, the Moulton-Barretts always celebrated birthdays and other festive occasions by writing odes and poems to one another. At least once this practice was revived in Wimpole Street. In the early 1840's a young distant cousin, Georgiana Elizabeth (Lizzie) Barrett, became the ward of EBB's father, because her mother was mentally unstable and her own father was in the West Indies. EBB wrote the ten-year-old girl a Valentine's Day poem in 1844—and had it embellished with decorations by Arabella—to reassure her that she was loved and to tell her that she was to consider Wimpole Street her home. Also shown is a drawing of Georgiana, probably done on her tenth birthday (22 June 1843), by Alfred Moulton-Barrett, whom she married in 1855. (Plate 5)

Robert Browning's Early Years

13. Robert Browning's Christening Robe

RB was baptized by the Revd. George Clayton at the York Street Independent Chapel, Walworth, on 14 June 1812. It is likely that the christening robe was made for this ceremony, as the fine lawn and the Scottish lace are contemporary. After being worn by Sarianna at her baptism, the robe was given to uncle Reuben Browning and used for his children; it remained in his family until recently. (Plate 6)

14. *Novum Jesu Christi Testamentum*, Limoges, 1812
Inscribed with RB's name by his mother, Sarah Anna Browning

RB's mother had strong evangelical beliefs. She persuaded her husband to leave the Church of England and attend the York Street church with her; she brought up her two children with firm Christian authority at home. It was, therefore, appropriate when young Robert was starting to learn Latin that she should give him this New Testament as a present.

15. Portrait of Robert Browning, Sr.
Pencil drawing by Sarianna Browning, ca. 1864

This drawing, made two years before the death of RB's father, shows him in a characteristic pose, sketching. It was drawn by his daughter Sarianna in Paris, where they were both living because of a court case for breach of promise twelve years earlier which had forced them to go abroad. RB's father, a scholarly, kind, artistic man, was a clerk in the Bank of England, but his real interests were in his library. Hundreds of his annotated books survive to show what a valuable education RB enjoyed at home in Camberwell. They also explain the origin of some of the recondite knowledge RB displays in his early poetry. Robert Browning, Sr. was an accomplished caricaturist; he amused his family with his grotesque drawings, often accompanied by witty commentary. (Plate 7)

16. Sarianna Browning
Oil by unknown artist, ca. 1834

RB's sister and confidante, Sarianna spent a life devoted to others, as did so many Victorian spinsters. In turn she cared for her father, her brother and her nephew Pen, from her mother's death in 1849 until her own death in 1903. She was self-effacing in public but had a good mind and strong opinions. This portrait, made when she was barely twenty, shows something of her strong, attractive personality which caused RB's friend Joseph Arnould to write, "She is marvellously clever—such fine clear animal spirits—talks much and well, and yet withal is so simply and deeply good-hearted that it is a real pleasure to be with her." (Plate 7)

17. Browning's juvenile poetry
Letter from Sarah Flower to W.J. Fox, 31 May [1827]

RB started writing poetry early and had completed a small volume of poems, *Incondita*, by the age of thirteen. He destroyed these romantic verses a few years later, but not before they had been seen by the sisters Eliza and Sarah Flower, wards of Unitarian minister W.J. Fox. Presumably one of the sisters copied them into an album, and Sarah also copied them in this letter to Fox. But for its chance survival, all RB's juvenile poetry would have been lost. The two poems—"The first born of Egypt" and "The Dance of Death" are imitations of Coleridge and Byron and have little merit. Even so, like EBB's early poems, they show a linguistic facility, as can be seen in these lines from "The first born of Egypt":

> I marked one old man with his only son
> Lifeless within his arms—his witherd hand
> Wandering oer the features of his child
> Bidding him from that long dreary sleep
> And lead his old blind father from the crowd
> To the green meadows—but he answer'd not
> And then the terrible truth flash'd on his brain
> —And when the throng rolld on some bade him rise
> And cling not so unto the dead one there,
> Nor voice nor look made answer—he was gone . . .

18. Donne, John, *Poetical Works*, Edinburgh, 1779 RB's annotated copy

RB bought this copy of Donne's poems in 1834, then read it and reread it during the next eight years before giving it to his friend Alfred Domett to take to New Zealand in 1842. Donne was a profound influence on Browning: images and ideas from the metaphysical poet occur in many of his works as late as the 1880's. Donne's daring wordplay and his casuistry also interested the young Browning and caused him to underline and mark his copy hundreds of times. Some poems received special attention, such as *The Progresse of the Soule*, which RB was later to quote in *The Two Poets of Croisic* (1878) with the comment:

> Better and truer verse none ever made . . .
> Than thou, revered and magisterial Donne.

The vellum binding on this copy, which converts three small volumes into one, was probably ordered by RB before he presented the book to Domett. He was not to be long without a copy of Donne's poetry, because in June 1842 Thomas Powell gave him *Poems on Several Occasions*. In 1872, A.B. Grosart dedicated his *Complete Poems of John Donne* to RB, thus honouring Browning's advocacy of the seventeenth-century writer. (Plate 6)

Catalogue number 20

19a. Library call slip

b. Proofsheets of *Paracelsus*, 1835

Paracelsus, RB's first successful work, published in August 1835, was written in six months, after his new French friend André Victor Amédée de Ripert-Monclar, had suggested the subject to him. He needed to do some quick research; and his father's library proved inadequate, as it lacked the great edition of Paracelsus's works edited by Bitiskius in Geneva in 1658. RB consulted this edition in the British Museum Reading Room. Meanwhile his father scoured the bookshops for a copy, but only succeeded in finding one on 29 December 1835—four months after the poem's publication. RB's mother was equally interested in the progress of the poem; before publication RB had a set of proofsheets bound and presented them to her. She later owned two copies of the first edition.

20. Ripert-Monclar, André Victor Amédée de, Portrait of RB Pencil drawing, 1837

RB wrote to Fanny Haworth 1 July 1837: "I don't know that I shall leave Town for a month: my friend Monclar grows piteous when I talk of such an event—I can't bear to leave him; he is to take my portrait today (a famous one he *has* taken!)—and very like he engages it shall be. I am going to Town for the purpose." The portrait referred to, which Monclar drew in RB's album on 1 July, was sold at the Sotheby sale of Browning possessions in 1913 and has disappeared. The "famous one" he took earlier in the year is the portrait shown. This is unsigned but endorsed on the back and larger than the album drawing. It shows RB as more delicate and sensitive than in other early likenesses. He is consciously a poet with shirt open at the collar. This informality was probably influenced by portraits of Shelley and by Monclar himself, who affected similar casual dress. Later portraits always show RB wearing a cravat.

21. Browning, Robert, *Sordello*, London 1840 Presentation copy to Thomas Carlyle

RB worked for five years on his poem *Sordello*, interrupting his labours to write *Strafford* and to visit Italy for the first time. Its hostile reception from the reviewers and its failure to sell were to haunt Browning for the rest of his life. *Sordello* unfairly became renowned for its obscurity. The copy displayed is of particular interest.

RB first knew Thomas Carlyle in the late 1830's, when Carlyle rode out regularly to the Brownings' new house at Hatcham and RB visited the sage at Chelsea. In spite of their different philosophies, the two men struck up a strong friendship which lasted until Carlyle's death. Carlyle recognized RB's powerful intellect, which he thought superior to Coleridge's. For him RB was one of the few men in England engaged in literature "from whom it was possible to expect something." Even so, Carlyle disliked *Sordello* and, having read it through critically, urged RB to desert poetry for prose.

22. The Browning House at Hatcham Drawing by Sarianna Browning, ca. 1845

When RB was in his mid-twenties the Brownings moved from Camberwell to Hatcham, a village on the southern outskirts of London. Mrs. Sutherland Orr described the attractions of this larger home: "The long, low rooms of its upper storey supplied abundant accommodation for the elder Mr. Browning's six thousand books. Mrs. Browning was suffering greatly from her chronic ailment, neuralgia; and the large garden, opening on to the Surrey hills, promised her all the benefits of country air. There were a coach-house and stable, which by a curious, probably old-fashioned, arrangement, formed part of the house, and were accessible from it." RB more enigmatically and simply called the house "a goosepie." The move brought the Brownings closer to uncle Reuben and also gave RB a pleasant room to write in. He stayed here with his parents until his marriage in 1846.

Courtship and Marriage

23. Barrett, Elizabeth Barrett, *Poems*, London, 1844

The publication of this two-volume work had a profound effect on EBB's life. She had been extremely busy during her early invalid years in Wimpole Street collaborating with R.H. Horne in two literary ventures and writing much poetry. She felt she had made "general progress in strength and expression" and the two volumes, published in August 1844, established her reputation. They were dedicated to her father:

> Somewhat more faint-hearted than I used to be, it is my fancy thus to seem to return to a visible personal dependence on you, as if indeed I were a child again; to conjure your beloved image between myself and the public, so as to be sure of one smile,—and to satisfy my heart while I sanctify my ambition, by associating with the great pursuit of my life, its tenderest and holiest affection.

The touching sympathy and submission of these lines delighted Edward Moulton-Barrett. An even greater delight was felt by RB when, reading through "Lady Geraldine's Courtship," he found himself among the modern poets Geraldine's lover read to her:

> . . . at times a modern volume,—Wordsworth's solemn-thoughted idyl,
> Howitt's ballad-dew, or Tennyson's enchanted reverie,—
> Or from Browning some 'Pomegranate,' which, if cut deep down the middle,
> Shows a heart within blood-tinctured, of a veined humanity!—

On 10 January 1845 RB wrote to EBB: "I love your verses with all my heart, dear Miss Barrett . . . I do, as I say, love these Books with all my heart—and I love you too."

24. Browning, Robert, *Bells and Pomegranates*, London, 1841–46

RB's annotated copy

The "Pomegranate" of "Lady Geraldine's Courtship" referred to RB's series of *Bells and Pomegranates*, eight small pamphlets of poems and verse plays he published between 1841 and 1846. The copy displayed is RB's own and has a number of corrections and alterations in his hand. The most interesting of these occur throughout *Colombe's Birthday*. RB has annotated the first page: "I made the alterations in this copy to suit some—I forget what—projected stage representation: not that of Miss Faucit, which was carried into effect long afterwards. R.B. Feb. 10 '77." Helen Faucit, who had acted in *Strafford* at Covent Garden and *A Blot in the 'Scutcheon* at Drury Lane, presented *Colombe's Birthday* at the Haymarket in April 1853. We know that RB didn't alter the text for this production, so the annotations were probably made between 1844 and 1846 when RB still considered himself a dramatist. Charles Kean had shown an interest in *Colombe's Birthday* before it was published, and RB might have hoped that he would reconsider the play *after* publication. (Plate 8)

25a. Edwin Hingston

Sketch by Alfred Moulton-Barrett, 13 September 1845

b. Buttons and Crests

Gilt embossed livery buttons and silver crests used by the Moulton-Barrett servants at Wimpole Street

RB paid his first visit to Wimpole Street on 20 May 1845, and the door was opened for him by Edwin Hingston. In the next sixteen months Hingston became a familiar figure. After EBB's departure he remained at Wimpole Street until Edward Moulton-Barrett's death. The Moulton-Barretts, like most upper middle-class families, lived with some style—so Hingston's livery was embellished with the family crests. These were the

Moulton spread-eagle on an orb and the Barrett gryphon rampant. The pineapple on the shoulder of the gryphon indicated that the family was among the original settlers of Jamaica. (Plate 14)

26. RB's Writing Portfolio

This simple leather-bound folder was used by RB in the 1840's while he was producing *Bells and Pomegranates* and corresponding with EBB. It has a number of inscriptions in RB's hand, including a quotation from EBB's early poem "The Past." RB cited this quotation back to her in a letter of 19 December 1845:

> She shall speak to me in places lone
> With a low and holy tone.
> Ay! when I have lit my lamp at night
> She shall be present with my sprite:
> And I will say, whate'er it be,
> Every word she telleth me!

Other quotations include "The possession eternal" in Hebrew, "Absent she both hears and sees him absent" (Virgil. *Æneid*, 4, 83) and "Every day" in Italian. Beneath these is a sketch of what appears to be a four-legged grasshopper or locust with a crowned human head. The meaning of the sketch (if indeed it has one) has not yet been fully explained. Other quotations above and below the sketch are "To the place" in Hebrew and "Upstream the headwaters of the sacred rivers flow" (*Medea*, 410) in Greek. The meaning of these jottings is not clear but they were apparently written at different times. (Plate 10)

27. EBB's criticism of Browning's poems
56 pages sent to RB in 14 instalments, bound in a copy of *Bells and Pomegranates* VII and VIII

During the early months of their friendship EBB sent comments and criticisms on RB's latest poems, which he was preparing for publication as numbers VII and VIII of the *Bells and Pomegranates* series. These show EBB as an enthusiastic admirer of her future husband's work. Often he adopted the changes she recommended, as in "The Tomb at St. Praxed's" which had already appeared in print in *Hood's Magazine*. EBB wrote:

> *The Tomb at St Praxed's*
>
> 'Old Gandolf *came me in*, despite my care,
> For a shrewd snatch &c'
>
> Is that 'came me in' a correct expression . . or rather, does it *express* . . does it not make the meaning hard to get at?
>
> This is a wonderful poem I think—& classes with those works of yours which show most power . . most unquestionable genius in the high sense. You force your reader to sympathize positively in his glory in being buried! And what a grand passage that is, beginning
>
> And then Lord I shall lie through centuries
> And hear the blessed mutter of the mass &c.
>
> (Plate 11)

28a. Inkstand

Used by EBB at Wimpole St. (Plate 11)

b. Three Letters

2 from EBB to RB, 10 September and 13 September 1846.
1 from RB to EBB, 12 September 1846.

c. Leather Case

Used by EBB for keeping the letters sent to her by RB. (Plate 12)

d. Marquetry Box

Used by RB for keeping the letters sent to him by EBB. (Plate 12)

The love letters of EBB and RB, that "extended conversation on paper," survive intact. These 573 letters, mostly written on small sheets of paper and enclosed in tiny envelopes, were carefully preserved by the recipients. Elizabeth kept RB's missives in a collapsible green leather case which she carried with her when she eloped. Robert put those from EBB in a brown marquetry box. When he burnt most of his personal correspondence in 1887, RB felt he couldn't destroy Elizabeth's letters and gave them to Pen, who published the whole correspondence in 1899. The three letters displayed have been chosen from the end of the series. The first, from EBB on 10 September 1846, asks Robert to call the following day so that final plans for their wedding might be made:

> Dear, dearest—take care, & keep yourself unhurt & calm. I shall not fail to you—I do not, I will not. I will act by your decision, & I wish you to decide. I was yours long ago, & though you give me back my promise at this eleventh hour, .. you generous, dear unkind!... you know very well that you can do as well without it– So take it again for my sake & not your own–

Catalogue number 34

Two hours after the secret wedding ceremony, when EBB had returned home, Robert wrote:

> Words can never tell you, however,—form them, transform them anyway,—how perfectly dear you are to me—perfectly dear to my heart and soul.
>
> I look back, and in every one point, every word and gesture, every letter, every *silence*—you have been entirely perfect to me—I would not change one word, one look–
>
> My hope and aim are to preserve this love, not to fall from it—for which I trust to God who procured it for me, and doubtlessly can perserve it.

The next day Elizabeth replied:

> Dearest, in the emotion & confusion of yesterday morning, there was yet room in me for one thought which was not a feeling—for I thought that, of the many, many women who have stood where I stood, & to the same end, not one of them all perhaps, not one perhaps, since that building was a church, has had reasons strong as mine, for an absolute trust & devotion towards the man she married,—not one!

29a. Netted Purse

Decorated with tassels and two rings. One ring is etched "Elizabeth Barrett to Robert Browning"; the other "Sept. 12th 1846 St. Mary le-bone Church." Given to RB by EBB as a memento of their wedding day. (Plate 17)

b. Necklace with Cross

Cross of black onyx, decorated with marcasite, silver and a central pearl, attached to a chain composed of black onyx rods and cylinders. Given to EBB by RB on their honeymoon. (Plate 17)

30. Hosmer, Harriet, The Brownings' Clasped Hands
Cast in plaster

Harriet Hosmer, a young American sculptor, pupil of Gibson, and friend of the Brownings, made a mould of their hands in Rome late in 1853. Various bronze castings exist, plus two known plaster castings including this one. (Plate 15)

The Years at Casa Guidi

Catalogue number 35a

31a. Browning, Robert, *Christmas-Eve and Easter-Day*, London, 1850

Composed by RB shortly after he and EBB settled at Casa Guidi, *Christmas-Eve and Easter-Day* was published on 1 April 1850. The copy on display was given by Browning to fellow-poet Leigh Hunt in August 1857.

b. Browning, Robert, *Poems*, Boston, 1850

Bearing the date 1850 though actually issued late in the previous year, this was the first American reprint of RB's *Poems*. In 1852 he gave the exhibited copy to Mrs. Anna Jameson, the friend who had accompanied the Brownings from Paris to Italy on their 1846 honeymoon trip.

32a. Story, William Wetmore, Bust of RB
Marble copy of terra-cotta bust, 1861

Story modelled the bust in Rome in May 1861 for EBB, who considered it "perfect." The Brownings had known the Story family for over ten years, and these families had spent time together in Florence and Bagni di Lucca as well as in Rome. RB had studied sculpture in Story's Rome studio in 1860. A marble copy of the bust was commissioned by George Moulton-Barrett in 1864 and given to Pen. The copy on display was made for Dr. A.J. Armstrong in the 1930's from the terra-cotta original at the Keats-Shelley house in Rome.

b. Story, William Wetmore, Posthumous Bust of EBB
Marble copy of terra-cotta bust, 1864

After EBB's death, Story created this bust as a companion to that of RB. The bust, which is an idealized likeness, like so much of Story's work, was copied in marble in the same year. This copy was made in the 1930's from the terra-cotta original.

33a. Photograph of RB
Mayer and Pierson, Paris, 2 June 1856

b. Letter from RB to James T. Fields, 20 October 1856

This, the earliest known photograph of Browning, was taken in Paris in June 1856 for his American publisher, J.T. Fields, who had requested a portrait for the frontispiece of a new volume of poems. In a letter to Fields of 18 June RB vividly describes sitting for the photograph:

> . . . one very hot day a fortnight ago I literally ran & got done for. It is on its way in M. Bossange's packet: I can only say that the artists are the first in repute here but they *retouch* & so far spoil, if friends' evidence may be received. I am unable to give an opinion but three or four competent judges agree that the eyes are good, the nose thickened overmuch, the mouth coarsened to match, *the folds of the coat capital.* I am responsible for all that Orson-like hair & beard,—both of which wanted trimming & got it next day. Still, there's inevitably *something* like.

The photograph did not reach Boston. Somewhere en route it was mislaid or stolen. Four months later, RB, who had been visiting London, wrote to Fields:

> This is indeed vexatious,—this loss of the photograph, since you care to have such a thing. I sate, as I told you, to Mayer and Pearson [*sic*], notable operatives in this way; and, myself, deposited the same with the people at M. Bossange's—explaining the use you intended it for: they engaged that you should receive it by their next parcel, for which (they said) I was just in time. I directed it myself, marked *très-fragile* on the outside wrapper, in short did all that should have been done—and the result is that you hear no more of the matter! . . . What can I do? We leave England to-morrow, or next day at latest—stay a single day at Paris,—stop, perhaps, at Florence. Can I do anything, sit again &c. &c[.]

In fact, Fields had no need to print a new edition, so the photograph wasn't urgently needed. Tentatively RB suggested a substitute —Woolner's medallion—and nothing more was heard of the missing photograph for almost 130 years. In August 1985 it unexpectedly reappeared in New York in its original mount, inscribed by RB on the reverse: "For James T. Fields, Esq. Boston. U.S. Taken at Paris, June 2. 1856." In spite of RB's comments about retouching, the photograph is remarkably life-like and invites comparison with the well-known portraits by Rossetti, Talfourd and Gordigiani. (Plate 16)

Catalogue number 35b

34. Woolner, Thomas, Portrait of RB Bronze medallion, 1856

The Pre-Raphaelite poet and sculptor Thomas Woolner worked on his medallion of RB in the summer of 1856 in London. He claimed that he had made it so like him that "folks have made a fuss over it, his wife seems not to know how to express enough praise." Certainly RB admired it, since he recommended it to J.T. Fields as a replacement for the lost Paris photograph:

> A young artist of great promise has just executed a particularly good profile of the face you are kind enough to want,—a medallion– Mr Hurlbert has a copy: the work has however been sensibly improved since his departure by a little scraping at the end of the nose—which was of the longest, it was thought.

William Bell Scott admired the workmanship, but called Browning's "the most unprepossessing poet's head it is well possible to imagine," while W.M. Rossetti commented:

> The quality of keenness . . . is strikingly apparent . . . Here the precise contour of the features is rendered with an exactitude and an emphasis for which a sculptured profile is a more positive document than art of other kinds can readily be. . . It is remarkable, considering that this is a work of sculpture, that the eye is made the most expressive feature of all; it seems to look, with a steady glance of scrutiny and almost of challenge, into men and things.

35. Photographs of RB
Alessandri, Rome, 1860 and 1861

a. In Siena in the autumn of 1859 RB changed his appearance by letting his beard and moustache grow together. EBB thought this most becoming and considered him "in very good look altogether." The photograph taken in Rome a few months later shows this newly trimmed beard and moustache. RB is wearing an ill-fitting wrinkled suit and seems to have come straight from working in Story's studio.

b. His hair cut much shorter than in 1860, RB poses the following year in Alessandri's studio with a painting of St. Peter's Basilica behind the table.

c. This is a detail of a photograph showing RB, hat in hand, standing in front of a backdrop of the Colosseum. It was presumably taken along with photographs of EBB dated 27 May 1861.

Catalogue number 35c

36a. Talfourd, Field, Portrait of EBB
Coloured chalk, 1859–69

b. Photograph of the Talfourd portrait, 1859
Signed by EBB

Field Talfourd (brother of RB's friend, the lawyer and writer T.N. Talfourd) made a drawing of EBB at the request of Ellen Heaton in Rome in March 1859. Miss Heaton commissioned the drawing to rival the painting of EBB by Gordigiani which had been commissioned by Sophia May Eckley the previous year. Each hoped to achieve the better likeness. EBB herself greatly liked the Talfourd drawing:

> Certainly it is a most exquisite work—rather a transfiguration than a literal likeness . . . Still people who have seen me only once, exclaim how like it is . . and the general opinion is perfectly in its favour!– There is a certain sadness, but it is quiet . . . and a look of the spirit's face in it which only a man of genius could give in a chalk drawing–

This version is now in the National Portrait Gallery, London, to whom RB wrote in 1868 describing it as "the best in existence, perhaps."

EBB was so pleased with the original drawing that she had it photographed and sent copies to her family and friends. The version on display was RB's copy. This second version is less finished, more life-like and more attractive to modern eyes. RB kept it until his death when it passed to Pen and was sold in the Sotheby auction of 1913. (Plate 19)

37. Copy of photograph of EBB
Probably Macaire, Le Havre, September 1858

The original was inscribed by EBB: "Elizabeth Barrett Browning for RB only—with all her love and very little likeness. Sept. 17. 1858." The date shows that the photograph was signed at Le Havre three days before the Brownings left for Paris. EBB is shown wearing the lace collar and cuffs which Henrietta had recently sent her from England. As there must have been few photographers in Le Havre at this period we may assume it to have been taken by Macaire, and the occasion to have been a sitting for a photograph requested by EBB's American publisher C.S. Francis. The inscription suggests that the Brownings considered it a failure, and so EBB sat again the next day (see No. 38). The original photograph was sold at Sotheby's in 1913 and later in 1963. Its present location is unknown.

38. Photograph of EBB

Copy by Elliot and Fry of detail from Macaire photograph, Le Havre, 18 September 1858

This was one of EBB's favourite photographs. Taken in Le Havre on 18 September 1858 after a previous unsuccessful sitting, it was sent to America for a head-and-shoulders engraving. A three-quarter-length portrait from the photograph was also engraved for the fourth edition of *Aurora Leigh* (see No. 90e). RB wrote to his publisher Edward Chapman on 19 September:

> I promised Francis a year ago a photograph of my wife—of which he means to make an engraving. You know, or don't know, that there have been certain horrible libels on humanity published as portraits of her in America: and I shall not be sorry to extinguish them—as the Photograph taken yesterday may be expected to do. It was executed by a clever man here, Warnod—and is so satisfactory that I keep it myself and only send a copy to Francis.

Warnod was presumably employed by Macaire, who had asked him to photograph EBB after his own initial failure. It is known that EBB disliked having her photograph taken and only submitted to please her husband.

Catalogue number 39

39. Portrait of EBB

Fine pen, ink and watercolour by unknown artist, ca. 1858

This copy of the Macaire photograph (18 September 1858) belonged to EBB's son, Pen Browning, who kept it beside his bed throughout his life. It is shown in the original frame.

40. Photographs of EBB

Alessandri, Rome, 1860 and 1861

EBB was photographed twice in Rome by Alessandri, in early Spring 1860 and on 27 May 1861. The first sitting she shared with Pen, and on the second she and RB were photographed separately. After her death RB had copies of the 1861 photographs made by Bingham of Paris and distributed them among his friends and relations and his domestic staff until the mid-1880's.

a. *1860, variant A:* Pen and EBB both sitting. Photograph formerly in the possession of Pen's wife, Fannie Browning.

b. *1860, variant B:* Pen standing, EBB sitting. Inscribed on verso by EBB: "Rome 1860."

c. *1861, variant A:* Presented by RB to Mr. and Mrs. James Martin, this photograph was taken a month before EBB's death.

d. *1861, variant B:* Presented by RB to Lady Cowper, to whom he dedicated *Balaustion's Adventure*.

41a. Pen Browning, *Certificat de Naissance et de Baptême*

b. Lock of Pen Browning's hair

Originally enclosed in a letter to Henrietta, 18 April 1849, when Pen was just over a month old

Robert Wiedemann Barrett Browning was born in Casa Guidi, Florence, on 9 March 1849, after a twenty-one-hour labour. EBB was unable to feed the baby, so a wet-nurse was quickly found. On June 26 the little boy was baptized in the Eglise Évangelique-Réformée. His second name "Wiedemann" (incorrectly spelled on the certificate) was RB's mother's maiden name, and it was from this that he began to be called Penini, which was shortened eventually to "Pen." The baptismal certificate gives the wrong date for the christening and is presumably a copy made for RB two days later. (Plate 20)

Catalogue number 40a

42. Photograph of Pen Browning as a child
Alessandri, Rome, 1860

Taken at the same time as 40 (a) and (b), this photograph was sent by EBB to Mrs. David Ogilvy with an inscription on the verso. (Plate 20)

43. Pen Browning as a child
Marble bust by Alexander Munro, 1859

A gift from RB to EBB. The bust was modelled in clay at Casa Guidi in the autumn of 1858 and was exhibited in marble in London the following year. It cost twenty-five guineas. This was equivalent to what the Brownings had paid for a year's rent on the Casa Guidi apartment when they first took it unfurnished in 1848, but EBB thought the price reasonable for such an "exquisite" portrait. Elizabeth Wilson, EBB's maid and Pen's bosom friend, was the only person to disagree; she thought the bust too melancholy. (Plate 20)

44. Holy Bible, London, 1846
Gift to Pen Browning from Margaret Fuller

This Bible with its poignant inscription was given to the child Pen by Margaret Fuller when she, her husband—the Marquis Ossoli, and their baby boy visited Casa Guidi on 5 May 1850. One of the leading transcendentalists of her day, Margaret Fuller Ossoli inscribed the book: "Robert Wiedeman Barrett Browning in memory of Angelo Eugene Philip Ossoli Florence, 1850, second year of their lives. God keep them pure both; and lead them to fulness of love and wisdom!" Two months later Margaret Fuller and her family were all drowned when the ship in which they were returning to America was wrecked off the New York coast.

45. Memorandum made while furnishing Casa Guidi
Signed by Robert Browning

The Brownings discovered the apartment on the first floor of Casa Guidi (opposite the Pitti Palace), their home during most of their married lives, on 18 July 1847. To begin with they rented the apartment furnished for two months. Next year the same rooms became available unfurnished for twenty-five guineas a year, so they signed a year's lease and moved in on 9 May 1848 with the barest essentials of furnishings and furniture. Then began a hunt through the antique-shops, markets and salerooms of Florence for chairs, sofas, carpets, chests and curtains. After three months RB turned his attention to pictures, mirrors and tapestries. Thus, by the beginning of 1849, Casa Guidi was stamped with the Brownings' own personality. Although the buying spree was over, they continued to acquire more antiques, books and furnishings during the ten remaining years at Casa

Guidi. RB in particular possessed a collector's eye and appetite and enjoyed finding a bargain.

Right-hand side of this exhibit item bears notation by RB about payment of 45 piastres, for five pieces of furniture including delivery.

46a. Teapot

Silver, engraved with EBB's initials; used by her at Casa Guidi.

b. Berlin Trembleuse Cup and Saucer

With floral initial "B," detached sprigs of flowers, and ribbon pattern in relief terminating in a knot handle. Used by EBB at Casa Guidi.

c. Tea Caddy

Mother-o'-pearl, finely engraved with landscape and decorative panels; fitted with lock and key, and having two compartments. Belonged to EBB at Casa Guidi. (Plate 18)

47a. Brooch

Gold, with intricate floral design and three amber topazes, given by RB to EBB on their first wedding anniversary. (Plate 17)

b. Italian Buttons

Set made of silver. Belonged to EBB in Florence. (Plate 19)

c. Mantilla

Black lace with floral pattern, two scalloped lace ties. Worn by EBB. (Plate 19)

d. Mittens

Black lace half-mittens, worn by EBB when attending chapel. (Plate 19)

e. Pencil

Gold chased, with Rose of France stone at end. Used by EBB throughout her years at Casa Guidi.

Catalogue number 40c

48a. Signet Ring

Band of 22-carat gold, set with a green bloodstone which bears intaglio of Browning crest and motto. Acquired by RB not long after his marriage and worn for the rest of his life. (Plate 26)

b. Passport.

Issued to RB by the Austrian Embassy in London in 1856, it also applied to EBB, their son, and their maid. This 20-page document provides a valuable record of the Brownings' travels during EBB's last years. Much of the Italian Peninsula, where they lived and travelled extensively, was controlled by Austria.

c. Calling Card Plate

Copper. Used for making RB's calling cards in Florence. Inscribed with his name and "Casa Guidi."

d. Calling Cards

Various cards left on the Brownings, including two from Charles Dickens and one from Tennyson. (Plate 16)

e. The Brownings' Calling Card

Only known sample of the only known card printed for *both* Brownings.

EBB left it on an unidentified recipient in London in 1856, with notation that she would be at home to visitors "Monday—between four & six." (Plate 16)

49a. Browning, Elizabeth Barrett and Robert, *Two Poems*, London, 1854
Presentation copy from EBB to the Revd. R.M. Hanna

The only joint publication of the Brownings, this 16-page pamphlet was written by them and specially printed by Chapman and Hall to assist EBB's sister Arabella in her efforts on behalf of the poor. Copies were offered for sale at a bazaar to aid a "Refuge for young destitute girls." On 30 March 1854 RB sent Chapman the manuscript of his "The Twins" and EBB's "A Plea for the Ragged Schools of London":

> Here are the poems. Will you kindly get two or three hundred copies struck off, in the simplest fashion, with as much taste as is consistent with cheapness—so that they may be sold, say, at sixpence a copy? No covers, you know, or anything but the plain sheetful, simply doubled into shape—making the best show you can for [the] little we want to spend.

It is unknown how many copies were printed and how many sold, but the pamphlet has had a troubled history. It was used as the model for a number of forgeries by T.J. Wise in the 1880's and 1890's, most particularly of EBB's "Runaway Slave at Pilgrim's Point." In 1887 a bundle of *Two Poems* was discovered, which sold at 2^s each. These were probably genuine—those left unsold at the 1854 bazaar; but it is possible that T.J. Wise and his confederates had facsimiles made and passed these off as the original pamphlets. Certainly far more than the original 200–300 ordered by RB are in circulation. As recently as 1980 an English bookseller had a cache of seventy-seven from the Buxton Forman estate, so the matter invites further investigation. The copy displayed is clearly genuine, as it is one of only four known presentation copies. Maxwell Hanna was a Scottish clergyman in Florence who preached interminably long Sunday sermons, which RB dutifully attended.

b. Autographs of the Brownings

On 21 October 1856, presumably to assist the Woman's Hospital in New York, EBB and RB jointly signed cards which were loosely inserted in copies of *Two Poems*.

50a. Mignaty, George, Drawing Room at Casa Guidi
Oil, painted shortly after EBB's death, 1861

b. Photograph of the Mignaty painting
RB's copy

The drawing room was the heart of Casa Guidi; here the Brownings entertained visitors, and EBB wrote her poetry and her letters. It was large (33′ x 20′) with high ceilings, a cool room of soft light, a refuge from the heat and glare of a Florence noon. T.W. Higginson described the Brownings' way of life here:

> They live in the most charming way, in a large old palace with a great parlor in which they sit in the evening; on the one side a large fireplace with an open fire, close to which sits Mrs. Browning, almost lost in a large armchair; on the opposite side sits her husband, and between them is a third chair for a guest, as they rarely have more than one at a time. On the opposite side

of the room are ranged her book shelves full of well-thumbed books including many Greek ones in rare editions. . . . The ends of the room are filled with pictures, quaint furniture, statuettes, and all kinds of things picked up by Browning in his all-observant rambles.

Another American, Kate Field, gave a more romantic picture:

> There was something about this room that seemed to make it a proper and especial haunt for poets. The dark shadows and subdued light gave it a dreamy look which was enhanced by the tapestry-covered walls and the old pictures of saints that looked out sadly from their carved frames of black wood. Large bookcases, constructed of specimens of Florentine carving selected by Mr. Browning, were brimming over with wise-looking books. Tables were covered with more gayly bound volumes, the gifts of brother authors. . . . A quaint mirror, easy-chairs and sofas, and a hundred nothings that always add an indescribable charm, were all massed in this room. But the glory of all, and that which sanctified all, was seated in a low arm-chair near the door. A small table, strewn with writing-materials, books, and newspapers, was always by her side.

Soon after EBB's death, RB wished to record the happy years at Casa Guidi. Having found the lighting in the drawing room unsuitable for photography, he invited George Mignaty, a Greek artist with an English wife, to paint an oil-sketch. He then had this photographed and sent to friends. (Plate 21)

51. Drawing Room Furnishings from Casa Guidi

The following items can be seen in the Mignaty painting. (Plate 21)

a. Haworth, E.F., *Pen Browning playing the piano*, ca. 1856

Oil on canvas. (Plate 24)

b. Italian School, *The Madonna*, ca. 1500

Oil on canvas. (Plate 23)

c. Plaque with head of Æschylus

Circular bronze with head in relief. (Plate 24)

d. Taper Stand

Bronze. (Plate 22)

e. Folding Chair

Mahogany, with plush seat and back support, elaborately carved. (Plate 21)

f. Fan

Dark green muslin with gold border, inscribed by EBB. (Plate 22)

52. Other Furnishings from Casa Guidi

a. Italian Escritoire, ca. 1650

Ornate carved wood with folding top, pull-down front and 12 drawers. Bought for Casa Guidi. (Plate 23)

b. Side Chair

Olive wood frame with wicker seat. One of a pair used at Casa Guidi. (Plate 23)

c. Murillo, Bartolomé Esteban, Two Children, Our Saviour and St. John, with a Lamb

Watercolour. (Plate 24)

d. Sienese School, Two Saints, ca. 14th or 15th century
Oil on wood. (Plate 24)

Elizabeth Barrett Browning's Death

53a. Letter from EBB to Arabella Moulton-Barrett, 19 September 1860

b. Lock of their sister Henrietta's hair, cut after death

At the beginning of the new decade EBB's frail constitution received two emotional shocks: her sister Henrietta's death on 23 November 1860 and the death of Count Camillo Benso Cavour in June 1861. Concern over Henrietta and over the Italian political situation can be seen in this letter which EBB wrote to her sister Arabella from Siena in September 1860. Depression and nervous tension are in evidence throughout:

> . . . how deeply I have been suffering from anxiety. In fact, I go on very well for a day or two or three or four even, after an account such as George sent me,—and then come the days for expectation of a letter when the anguish grows too heavy sometimes– The post comes about eight in the morning . . and I wind up my affairs at night as I was to be shot at that hour– It has been terrible. . . . But none of you can have had a more dismal summer than I– I dont feel as if I had had a summer at all– Italian affairs indeed have kept power to stir me—& they would do the same if I lay on my deathbed– No private grief or suffering could prevent the swelling of my heart in sympathy, with the liberated people, while it beats at all[,] and the crisis is terrible just now . . . There is a great standard figtree, like a forest tree, under my window, and I get out to sit there for hours sometimes with books & newspapers . . & the worm pricking all the while through every thought as it arises.

During the writing of the letter, EBB received better news of the Italian struggle, which—in her excitement—she crammed into the inside of the envelope:

> So—Ancona not taken after all—but Lamoriciere beaten– It is great news. The withdrawal of Napoleon's ambassador *means nothing*—an evasion for the "Powers". He will stand by us to the last . . . Best of loves to all– Love me dear darling—Your Ba—*Write*.

The excitement and worry of these months caused EBB's strength to fail.

54. Letter from RB to Mr. and Mrs. David Ogilvy, 29 July 1861

On 29 June at half past four in the morning EBB died in RB's arms. Before leaving Florence for the last time, RB sent their friends the Ogilvys this account of her death:

> There was no pain,—above all, no least expectation of the parting which to her would have been the cruelest of pains. She was sure up to the last that the attack differed in nothing from the many she had recovered from. I believed this to a certain degree, but (as it now seems to me) disbelieved it at the bottom of my soul. Your old acquaintance Dr. Wilson was called in for the first time,—he looked gravely at the symptoms,—she reassured me—"The way with them all,—so I was told all those years ago,—what is there new in hearing that my lungs are affected? You will see!" . . . She went into the presence of God fearless as his own child, that she was. I could have wished no better for her or myself, if the end *was* to be.

55a. Altham, William Surtees (*né* Cook), Diary
Four volumes, 1844–45, 1847–87

b. Newspaper obituaries

When the news of EBB's death reached England the newspapers were generous in their praise of her poetic achievements. The Italian press hailed her as a champion of her adopted country, and the municipality of Florence placed a plaque—expressing Florentine gratitude—above the door of Casa Guidi. Henrietta's widower, William Surtees Cook, sadly recorded her death in his diary on 6 July:

> My sister Elizabeth Browning, the poet[,] died at Florence Saturday June 29– My precious one's own dearest Ba—gone to join her! My own darling you are spared the pain of that terrible hearing—"Ba is no more!"– The papers were full of it—and I had heard nothing. Poor dear Arabel your heart is bleeding terribly! I know–

(Plate 25)

56. Photograph of EBB's Tomb
Sent to James Martin by RB in 1867

EBB was buried in the Protestant Cemetery, Florence, on 1 July. In 1862 Frederic Leighton designed a monument for her grave, consisting of a sarcophagus supported by six pillars. The marble sarcophagus bears a central medallion depicting an idealized head of Poetry. RB was most enthusiastic and intended to go to Florence for the unveiling. Sadly, things went wrong. The design drawings were sent to a young English artist in Florence, Count Henry Cottrell, who was made responsible for seeing that they were carried out in the best marble. He and Italian advisors and workmen questioned the designs and made changes. Leighton, on a visit to Florence in 1864, was appalled and demanded that much of the work be done again. Eventually, in 1865, the monument was placed above EBB's grave. RB never revisited Florence to see this monument; but he was pleased with photographs of it, one of which he kept framed in his study. In 1866 he wrote to George Moulton-Barrett, who had visited Florence:

> For the monument,—I am simply rejoiced that you like it. You know it was just what I was able to accomplish in that direction, and no more: I mean,—that had it been of pure gold it would have gone no farther in the way of being a *fit* offering,—and, on the other hand, if my circumstances had only allowed me to put up a wooden cross, *that* would have sufficed. But I was fortunate in the sympathy of Leighton, and so, I hope, have been able perhaps to manage that the little which *is* done, is on the whole well done. . . . by the photographs, I judge that Leighton's work is adequately rendered,—and we must be content.

Content he couldn't be, because in 1875 vandals and souvenir-hunting tourists damaged the tomb. Once again he and Leighton had to resist changes proposed by Italian experts—this time the substitution of black for white marble. Repairs were made and the monument still survives today, much as Leighton planned it. (Plate 25)

57. Hart, Joel Tanner, "On the death of Mrs. Elizabeth Barrett Browning"
Ms. dated Florence, 2 July 1861

Joel Tanner Hart, American sculptor with a studio in Florence, commemorated EBB with a poem of seven stanzas, the first of which reads:

> Not thine alone Brittania, nor alone
>   Columbia's tears shall balm her sacred Urn;
> But sorrows flow where e'er, from zone to zone,
>   Religion smiles, or freedom's altars burn.

Robert Browning's Later Life

58a. Photograph of 19 Warwick Crescent, ca. 1890

b. Sanderson, Arthur, View from RB's study, Warwick Crescent

Watercolour, 1890. (Plate 26)

c. Commemorative Plaque

Placed on 19 Warwick Crescent ca. 1890 to record RB's tenure. (Plate 26)

In May 1862 RB moved into 19 Warwick Crescent in Paddington, which was to remain his home until 1887. He chose the area because it was near his sister-in-law, Arabella Moulton-Barrett. The house was modest but well-built, near the end of a terrace. (Joaquin Miller when he came to visit thought RB owned the whole terrace.) The house overlooked the Grand Junction Canal and a small wooded island in the centre of the turning basin. Visitors likened it to Venice; but, to begin with, RB found it a dreary and unwelcome contrast to Italy. The furniture from Casa Guidi, looking rather clumsy in the smaller rooms, was a constant reminder of what he had left behind.

59. Moscheles, Felix, RB's study, January 1890

Engraving of a lost watercolour commissioned by Pen after RB's death

Some of the Italian furniture can be seen in this print of RB's study in his final London home, 29 De Vere Gardens. In particular, the chair to the right of the picture has a similar position in the Mignaty painting of Casa Guidi (50a). The large bookcase, too, is one of those bought in Italy. Both are mentioned in the memoir of RB's valet, William Grove:

> Browning had two bookcases in his study, one a very large carved one in which he kept all of his most cherished volumes including Plato, Shelley and many other classical writers. This bookcase was usually crammed full with books[,] some shelves being lined two deep. There was also a special chair in his study which always stood on the right hand side of his own chair. Nobody was ever allowed to sit on this chair and to prevent anyone from doing so he would keep a pile [of] books on the seat[,] including a volume of poems by Mrs Barrett Browning. This was her favourite chair when alive which was the reason why he held it rather sacred.

The idea for the watercolour probably came from Luke Fildes's famous painting "The Empty Chair" (1870), which shows Charles Dickens's study at Gad's Hill immediately after his death. The Mignaty painting of Casa Guidi was clearly another influence.

60a. Antique marble head

This item, representing a lady, is from RB's collection and appears atop bookcase in No. 59. (Plate 27)

b. Pedestal Writing Table

Used by RB at Warwick Crescent and De Vere Gardens, this is the most prominent item in the Moscheles drawing (No. 59). The table is equipped with 12 drawers, two-fronted, and inlaid with black leather. It may have belonged to RB's father who, upon removing to Paris in 1852, had asked his son to store a writing table for him at London.

61. Browning, Robert, *Dramatis Personæ*, London, 1864

Dramatis Personæ, the first book RB published after his return to England, was also his first book to go into a second edition. Stimulated by the publication of a three-volume *Collected Poems* and a *Selections* (chosen by John Forster and Barry Cornwall), there was a flurry of interest in RB's poetry in 1864. Publication of a second edition of *Dramatis Personæ* enabled him to make some textual corrections. The major change was the addition of three stanzas to "Gold Hair" at the suggestion of George Eliot, who found the character motivation difficult to understand. The copy shown is RB's own, in which he made his annotations for the printing of the second edition. (Plate 27)

62. Gilchrist, Alexander, *Life of William Blake*, London, 1863
Presented to RB from the author's widow

A page of this early work on Blake bears a quotation from "Pictor Ignotus," indicative of the influence Browning was having on his fellow artists. Inserted is a letter from Mrs. Gilchrist expressing her wish that the poet have this copy of her late husband's work.

63. Browning, Robert, *Poetical Works*, London, 1868, 6 vols.
Volume 1, a presentation copy to Mrs. Nixon

In 1867 RB changed publishers. With the advent of George Smith of Smith, Elder & Co., his literary fortunes rose: sales increased and his books were properly advertised. The publication of the six-volume *Poetical Works* followed by *The Ring and the Book* constituted a major event. In eighteen months RB's poetry became readily available to the public in neat well-printed editions. With improved marketing the books cost less than the earlier editions from Chapman and Hall. Even the title-pages had a new look, with the proud announcement of two distinctions recently conferred on RB—Honorary M.A. of Oxford University and Honorary Fellow of Balliol College, Oxford. This volume was given to Mrs. Nixon, the wife of an artist friend. She wrote out RB's "Deaf and Dumb" on the back end-paper—five months before publication. Presumably the poem was shown her by sculptor Thomas Woolner, whose statue is mentioned therein.

64. Diploma of Oxford University
Document on vellum conferring the Degree of M.A., metal box with the arms of the University attached, 1867

RB had little formal education and no university degree. His honorary M.A. resulted from the efforts of his friend Benjamin Jowett, Master of Balliol College, who told RB in 1867:

> I have seen John Griffiths the keeper of the Archives who proposed in the Council the M.A. by Diploma. He begs me to assure you that this is not

> a lower but a much higher honour than the D.C.L.[,] hardly given since Dr Johnson's time except to Kings & Royal Personages.

RB was awarded the degree on 26 June 1867 and the following October was elected Honorary Fellow of Balliol. He was created D.C.L. in 1882. (Plate 29)

65a. Robe for Doctor of Civil Law at Oxford

b. Mortarboard

RB received his Oxford doctorate at the Encaenia of June 1882. There was much amusement in the Sheldonian Theatre when undergraduates let down a red cotton night-cap over the poet's head when he was being presented with his degree. RB later let Pen paint his portrait wearing the doctoral robe. He presented this portrait—one of Pen's best—to Balliol, where it hangs now in the College Library. RB wore the robe for the last time on 5 July 1889 when he dined at Lord Rosebery's to meet the Shah of Persia. (Plates 21 and 29)

66. Taunt, Henry, The Vice-Chancellor's Procession Photograph, inscribed by RB: "June 30. '86. Balliol, Oxford. RB."

In 1886 Benjamin Jowett completed his four-year term as Vice-Chancellor of Oxford University. RB went to Oxford for the Commemoration ceremonies, which included a luncheon in Balliol College Hall (hosted by Jowett who was Master) and ended with a fireworks display in the evening. The photograph shows the university procession leaving the recently built Balliol Hall. Jowett follows the two bedels and leads the main academic procession, which includes RB. On this occasion RB would have seen his portrait, painted by Pen, which had been hung in the Hall three months before. (Plate 29)

67. Browning, Robert, *The Agamemnon of Æschylus*, London, 1877

Presentation copy to Professor Blackie

RB's one foray into the world of classical scholarship was his translation of Æschylus's *Agamemnon* in 1877. His pedantically literal and stilted translation was criticised by almost everyone, including Professor John Stuart Blackie to whom RB gave this copy. Blackie, professor of Greek at Edinburgh University, who had himself published a metrical translation of Æschylus in 1850, wrote honestly to RB:

> My dear poet & Hellenist:
>
> It was very kind in you to send me your Agamemnon with your own initials written with your own hand, especially as you perhaps knew, that in the field of translation I belonged to a different school: and there could be little hope of converting such a white-haired old rhymer to a new creed. I consider a *literal* & *rhythmical* translation of poetry, as a thing æsthetically perverse, and which should not be attempted. If a literal translation is wanted let it be done in prose.

After reading the play, Professor Blackie wrote in his copy:

> Like a lame ass that dances with the Graces
> Moves Browning here, not with his native paces.

68a. Cameron, Julia Margaret. Photograph of RB, 1870
RB's copy, mounted in an oval frame

b. Copy of Julia Margaret Cameron's photograph with attached signature of RB, owned by Anne Thackeray

Julia Margaret Cameron was the greatest society photographer of her day, remembered particularly for her portraits of Tennyson and her photographic illustrations for his *Idylls of the King*. She persuaded RB to sit for her in 1870. Swathing him in a cloak, Mrs. Cameron kept him waiting in acute discomfort for nearly two hours while she busied herself searching for the right parts of her camera and the right angles. The finished product shows RB more like an intrepid, triumphant explorer than a poet. It is the most robust of all his likenesses—more Mrs. Cameron's interpretation of her sitter than RB himself. A second photograph, full-face, taken at the same time, is more honest, and betrays some of RB's impatience at the length of the sitting. RB undoubtedly liked the first photograph and had a number of smaller copies made for friends. He gave the exhibited one to Anne Thackeray (the novelist's daughter), to whom he dedicated *Red Cotton Night-Cap Country*.

Catalogue number 68b

69. Browning, R.W.B., Portrait of RB, 1882
Oil on canvas

Painted early in 1882, this picture was purchased by RB's publisher George Smith. Pen was having difficulties in selling his work and so RB persuaded Smith to give the young man some encouragement:

> Come,—will you give One Hundred Guineas for the Portrait and all rights connected with it? If so, it is cheerfully yours. . . . I should like the picture to remain here till he [Pen] arrives in the course of a week or two—so as to give him the opportunity of retouching any little matter that he may hope to amend.

Later in the year, when Smith had purchased the painting, RB wrote again:

> Could you have the kindness to allow M. Rodin (the Sculptor) to see the Portrait in case it is at Waterloo Place? Pen is desirous that his Master should judge of it.

70. Browning, R.W.B., Portrait of Joseph Milsand
Oil on canvas

This is a companion-piece to No. 69, painted and framed at the same time, when Milsand was visiting London. RB kept it until his death, and it was sold at Sotheby's in 1913 for £1.10s. For Milsand, see Nos. 116–118. (Plate 28)

71a. Browning, Robert, *Fifine at the Fair*, London, 1872
Presentation copy to D.G. Rossetti

Inscribed "To Dante Gabriel Rossetti from his old admirer and affectionate friend. RB. June 4. '72." At the time of presentation, Rossetti fancied himself the target of a conspiracy by various other literary people. Upon receiving this copy of *Fifine*, he read certain lines which convinced him that RB had joined his supposed enemies. Literally hurling away the book, he broke off a 25-year friendship.

Catalogue number 69

b. Browning, Robert, *Red Cotton Night-Cap Country*, London, 1873
Corrected proofs

RB and Sarianna spent the summers between 1865 and 1875 holidaying in Northern France. They went to sea-side resorts in Brittany and Normandy, where RB learned to swim and enjoyed the bathing. Sometimes Pen accompanied them; almost always Joseph Milsand came up from Dijon to join them for a week or two. The holidays provided material for three books: *Fifine at the Fair*, *The Two Poets of Croisic* and *Red Cotton Night-Cap Country*. The first two portray well the Breton scenery RB encountered at Pornic and Le Croisic:

> Croisic, the spit of sandy rock which juts
> Spitefully northward, bears nor tree nor shrub
> To tempt the ocean, show what Guérande shuts
> Behind her, past wild Batz whose Saxons grub
> The ground for crystals grown where ocean gluts
> Their promontory's breadth with salt: all stub
> Of rock and stretch of sand, the land's last strife
> To rescue just a remnant for dear life.

As a modern photograph shows, Batz remains essentially the same today, a small town surrounded by salt flats. *Red Cotton Night-Cap Country* owed its being to St. Aubin in Normandy, and to a true story that Milsand told Browning when they were staying there—about a man of the district who committed suicide by throwing himself off a tower. RB wrote the poem using the real names of people concerned in the tragedy—but, fearing the strict libel laws, changed the names in proof. A proof copy is shown with a number of corrections in RB's hand. This represents an intermediate stage of revision. In many places RB has altered the name of the protagonist from the original Antoine Mellerio to the clumsy Antoine Hammario. He was eventually to adopt the name Leonce (Alphonse) Miranda.

72a. Match Box

In shape of a fish. Given to RB by Alfred Moulton-Barrett on the latter's return from Hong-Kong. (Plate 16)

b. Silver Paper Knife

Used by RB in Venice. Bought at Tiffany's of New York and given to RB by Pen and Fannie Browning. (Plate 29)

c. Gloves, Collar Tie and Cravat

Worn by RB. Given by Katharine Bronson to Balliol College, Oxford. (Plate 29)

d. Dressing Case

Belonged to RB. Given by Fannie Browning to RB's former valet and photographer, W.H. Grove. (Plate 29)

e. Grove, William H., "My Memories of Robert Browning," typed ms., ca. 1910

Grove entered Browning's service in 1875 and was a member of the household for approximately 10 years, prior to establishing a photographic studio. These recollections were recorded shortly before his death at the request of Mary M. Hubbard, to whom he presented the previous item.

73. Writing Portfolio
Containing blotting paper, penwiper and list of corrections to *Poetical Works* (1888–1889)

In 1887 RB and George Smith made plans for a new edition of RB's *Poetical Works* in 16 volumes, to be issued monthly during 1888 and 1889. RB revised the text, and the first volume was published in April 1888. Although the text of the new edition was intended to be definitive, a few errors crept in; so, before the early volumes were reissued in 1889, RB made further corrections. In this leather portfolio is an eight-page list of corrections in RB's hand for volumes IV–X of the 1888–89 edition. These were submitted to Smith in August 1889 just before RB left England for Italy. They are the last alterations he made to the text of his poems, because he died before he could amend volumes XI–XVI.

74a. Photograph of Wedding Party, Marriage of Pen and Fannie Browning, 1887

b. Photograph of Pen and Fannie on honeymoon

Pen married Fannie Coddington—a wealthy American—at Pembury, near Tunbridge Wells, on 4 October 1887. He was 38 and his bride 34. She had refused him in 1873, and it was clear that she was neurotic. In spite of all this, RB had great hopes for the marriage, which started well. Pen and Fannie decided to live in Venice and purchased the Ca' Rezzonico on the Grand Canal. In the photograph RB and Sarianna are shown to the left, Sarianna sitting and RB standing. To the left of Sarianna sits Marie Coddington, Fannie's sister, whose possessiveness contributed to the breakdown of the marriage.

75. Browning, R.W.B., Venetian Scene
Oil on canvas, 1888

Pen painted this Venetian side-canal while waiting to move into the Ca' Rezzonico. RB and Sarianna frequently visited Venice on holiday in the 1880's, but Pen's first visit there as an adult wasn't until 1885. He fell in love with the city and determined to make it his home.

76. Ca' Rezzonico, Venice
Two photographs, ca. 1890, during Pen's residence

Ca' Rezzonico is one of the largest palaces on the Grand Canal. Built in 1680, for the family of Pope Clement XIII, it contains ceilings by Giordano and Tiepolo. When Pen bought the Rezzonico it was in need of major redecoration. Within five years he successfully restored it to its former glory, and made it a comfortable home. Photograph of the drawing room shows Pen's painting "The Tanner's Garden" on the rear wall. Like so many of Pen's works, this and the large portrait of his father had been executed on a scale suitable for the grand rooms of the Rezzonico and blended well with older furniture and works of art.

Catalogue number 77

77. Giles, Godfrey Douglas, Portrait of RB
Pencil on card, dated 24 November 1889

Godfrey Giles, a former army officer turned artist, was staying with Pen and Fannie at the Rezzonico in November 1889. Miss Evelyn Barclay, another guest, described the occasion of the drawing:

> That afternoon Mr. Giles was sketching. Mr. Browning said, "Come now, Giles, do me." In a few minutes he had done a pencil sketch which was the last thing done of him. That evening I asked him to write his name below it, which he did–
>
> Here I'm gazing, wide awake,
> Robert Browning, no mistake!
>
> And said to Mr. Giles next day, "Now you have an unpublished work of mine." He was most cordial and kind in doing anything of that kind, always making it appear as if he were receiving a favour instead of granting it.

78. Barclay, Evelyn, Diary

Evelyn Barclay recorded the events of the last fortnight of RB's life in her diary. Although this differs in some particulars from Fannie Browning's account, it is probably the more accurate of the two. Walking on the Lido in damp weather, RB contracted bronchitis. His failing heart wasn't strong enough to withstand the illness and he died on 12 December. Just before he lost consciousness he was shown the first copy of his new book, *Asolando*:

> All day telegrams came pouring in. At 6:30 he again had a collapse from which he never really rallied. A telegram came at that moment saying that the first edition of his book was all sold. Pen bent over him and told him and he said, "More than satisfied. I am dying. My dear boy. My dear boy." When Cini came at 7 he said it would all be over in an hour, but he just breathed until 10 o'clock and then passed away without a struggle.

(Plate 30)

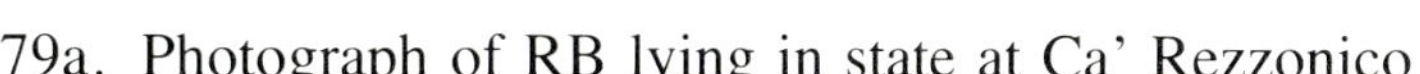

79a. Photograph of RB lying in state at Ca' Rezzonico

b. Lock of RB's hair
Cut after death by Fannie Browning and given to Evelyn Barclay

RB's body lay in state for a day in the hall on the first floor of the Rezzonico. There was a short service attended by his close friends before removal of the coffin to the chapel of San Michele, the Venetian Island of the Dead. As the Protestant Cemetery in Florence—burial place of EBB—was no longer used, RB's body was taken back to England and buried in Westminster Abbey on 31 December. (Plate 30)

80. Service sheet, ticket and other memorials of RB's funeral

The Abbey ceremony was organized by RB's publisher friend George Smith. The service, in Poets' Corner, was impressive—with a boy soprano singing EBB's poem "The Sleep" in a setting by John Frederick Bridge. Among the pall-bearers were Benjamin Jowett, Frederic Leighton, Hallam Tennyson and George Smith. (Plate 30)

81a. *Fortnightly Review*, NS vol. 47, January 1890

b. Story, William Wetmore, "Robert Browning"

Tributes to RB flooded the newspapers and magazines. Algernon Charles Swinburne composed a sequence of seven sonnets between 13–15 December, which he published in *The Fortnightly Review*:

> A graceless doom it seems that bids us grieve:
> Venice and winter, hand in deadly hand,
> Have slain the lover of her lovely strand
> And singer of a storm-bright Christmas Eve.

A closer friend, William Wetmore Story, sent his manuscript poem to Pen and Fannie:

> It scarcely seems, dear Friend you can be gone–
> Your voice still lingers in my ear—that tone
> So clear & quick it scarce could wait to say
> Your eager thought in our prosaic way,
> But leaped oer critic rules, assured that we
> Could follow where you leaped so easily,
> Still pressing on in thought, stopped by no gaps
> Of Broken phrasing—careless of all lapse–
>
> Dead? No!—Not dead! You never can be dead–
> Gone?—Yes—gone from us—from this brief Life fled
> But living still—& full of strength & fire
> Going forever onward—higher—higher
> In the new gladness of some purer sphere
> Beyond our reach . . .

82a. *The Browning Collections. Catalogue of Oil Paintings, Drawings & Prints; Autograph Letters and Manuscripts; Books; Statuary, Furniture, Tapestries, and Works of Art; the Property of R.W. Barrett Browning, Esq.*, London, 1913

Fannie Browning's copy

b. Moulton-Barrett, Edward A., [Notes on Pen's Estate]

Upon RB's death, his and his wife's library and effects were carefully preserved by Pen Browning. Apparently it was his intention to place them in Casa Guidi, which he purchased in 1893, and establish there a permanent memorial to his parents. Unfortunately he did not implement such a plan prior to his death, 8 July 1912.

After Pen's death there was a period of some confusion. Fannie Browning —separated from her husband for a number of years—claimed most of the estate. Pen's maternal cousins, the Moulton-Barretts, had their interests to maintain. The responsibility of representing the Moulton-Barretts' interests fell to Col. Edward Alfred Moulton-Barrett, eldest son of EBB's brother Alfred. His pivotal involvement in settling the estate is recorded in the form of notes, written on various slips of paper and stationery during his visit to Florence in August 1912.

It was eventually declared that Pen had died intestate, and the administrators of the estate were able to order his effects sold. On 1 May 1913 Messrs. Sotheby, Wilkinson and Hodge commenced a six-day sale of the Browning collections. The resulting dispersal of Browningiana has ever since been regarded, by Browning scholars and devotees, as a disaster.

THEIR ART

WORKS OF ROBERT BROWNING

PAULINE, 1833

83a. Browning, Robert, *Pauline*, London, 1833
One of only twenty-three known surviving copies of the first edition.

b. Shelley, Percy Bysshe, *Miscellaneous Poems*, London, 1826
RB's annotated copy, given to him by James Silverthorne, ca. 1826.

c. Hunt, Marianne, Bust of Shelley
Plaster, owned by RB. (Plate 26)

d. Fox, Eliza, Portrait of Eliza Flower
Pencil and crayon.

e. Unknown artist, Jemima Smith Browning
Miniature of RB's half-aunt.

f. Allingham, William, Commonplace Book
With transcript of letter from RB to Dante Gabriel Rossetti, 10 November 1847, concerning *Pauline*.

RB always disparaged *Pauline*. At different times he called it absurdly pretentious, an eyesore, an abortion, written "in juvenile haste and heat." He unsuccessfully tried to suppress the book and, having failed, reluctantly allowed it to be reprinted in 1868 and 1888 in slightly modified form. Yet the poem does not deserve such obloquy. It is RB's autobiography in verse, outlining his struggle with religious doubt during his late adolescence.

Published when he was twenty-one, *Pauline* is described on its title-page (a) as "A Fragment of a Confession." RB's later attempts to describe the poem as a form of dramatic monologue are not convincing; it is too strongly based on his own youthful feelings and has too many references to his reading and early life.

Pauline expresses RB's admiration for Shelley:

> Yet, sun-treader, all hail! From my heart's heart
> I bid thee hail!

He came across Shelley's poetry as early a 1826 when his cousin, James Silverthorne, gave him a copy of *Miscellaneous Poems* (b) which he eagerly read and annotated. He later wrote in this copy: "The foolish markings and still more foolish scribblings show the impression made on a boy by this first specimen of Shelley's poetry." However foolish he may have thought his juvenile scribblings to have been, RB always retained a respect for Shelley's poetry and also treasured a bust of the poet (c), made by Leigh Hunt's wife and given to him by Thomas Carlyle. This had been intended to adorn Shelley's grave in Rome; but it had been rejected by the Shelley family, who required a more handsome portrait.

Who was Pauline? Mrs. Sutherland Orr believed her to have been Eliza Flower (d), a close friend of W.J. Fox. Mr. Fox wrote the only favourable review of the poem. A more recent contender is Jemima Browning (e), RB's half-aunt only a year older than he, who lived nearby and who shared some of his boyhood with him. The Pauline of the poem is, however, such a shadowy figure that she is more an idealized woman than a real person. *Pauline* itself is a strongly romantic poem, vague in places, but containing passages of youthful enthusiasm and beauty. It greatly appealed to the young Dante Gabriel Rossetti when he read the anonymous book at the British Museum in 1847, after which he wrote to RB: "It seemed to me, in reading this beautiful composition, that it presents a noticeable analogy in style and feeling to your first acknowledged work, 'Paracelsus'." RB had to confess (f) and the secret was out. But for Rossetti's chance discovery and well-grounded suspicion, *Pauline* might have languished unknown and forgotten.

STRAFFORD, 1837

84a. Browning, Robert, *Strafford*, London, 1837

First edition, dedicated to William Charles Macready

b. Prompt copy of *Strafford*

First edition—presented to James Parsloe, prompter at Covent Garden —bound with prompt copies of T.N. Talfourd's *Ion* and J.S. Knowles's *The Daughter* and *The Hunchback*. *Strafford* has less annotation than the other three plays. Parsloe presumably used a manuscript copy for the first night. When *Strafford* proved a failure, he entered few comments to the printed text because it wouldn't be needed for use in the theatre.

c. Playbills for *Strafford*

First and second issues, from RB's library. Although *Strafford* is a full-length play of five acts, two other plays were performed the same evening. This was common Victorian practice; farces, operettas and melodramas were provided as light relief for a serious play. Reduced prices were available for those who wished to attend only the second part of the evening's entertainment.

d. Helen Faucit

Signed carte-de-visite photograph of detail from painting of Helen Faucit, as Antigone, by Frederic Burton.

e. Review of *Strafford* from *The Casket*, 13 May 1837

"Write a play, Browning, and keep me from going to America!" These words of William Charles Macready in 1836 set RB's poetic career along a wrong path. RB was not a natural dramatist; and *Strafford*, the first play he wrote for the great theatre manager, was unsuccessful. The subject of Charles I's favourite, Thomas Wentworth, Earl of Strafford, suggested itself because RB had been helping John Forster with a prose life of this man. The play was too full of talk: RB's intention of presenting Action in Character instead of Character in Action deprived *Strafford* of much theatrical power. Macready was gloomy after a first reading of the manuscript and grew progressively gloomier during rehearsals. ("Would it were over! It must fail—and it grieves me to think that *I am so placed*.") He altered and cut the play so much that RB made sure the full text was published (a and b) on the day *Strafford* was first presented at Covent Garden, 1 May 1837.

Strafford ran for only four nights. The first was Macready's benefit night and the theatre was full of his friends. In spite of a "puff" in the play-bills (c) that the play had been "indeed most eminently successful, and greeted with most enthusiastic fervour, by a house densely crowded in every part," attendances fell off and *Strafford* was withdrawn. Macready's performance in the title role and the performance of Helen Faucit (d) as Lady Carlisle were praised by the critics; but other actors were mediocre, the sets tawdry and the costumes poor (e). Ultimately, *Strafford*'s failure must be attributed to the play itself. For once the critics were justified; RB's genius lay elsewhere.

"The Pied Piper of Hamelin," 1842

85a. Browning, Robert, *Bells and Pomegranates, No. III, Dramatic Lyrics*, London, 1842

Contains the first printing of "The Pied Piper of Hamelin."

b. Wanley, Nathaniel, *Wonders of the Little World*, London, 1678

Verstegen, Richard, *A Restitution of Decayed Intelligence*, London, 1628

Melander, Otto, *Jocoseria*, 1626

Three books which RB knew from boyhood were sources for "The Pied Piper" and many other poems. *Jocoseria* suggested the title of RB's 1883 volume and was first mentioned in a note to *Paracelsus* (1835).

c. Macready, William C., Jr., Three drawings and letter to RB, 18 May 1842

d. Letter from RB to H. Courthope Bowen, 7 November 1881

e. Browning, Robert, *The Pied Piper of Hamelin*, illustrated by Kate Greenaway, London, [1889]

"The Pied Piper" was lucky to reach print. RB had no intention of publishing the poem, but was persuaded to do so by his sister Sarianna when he found himself short of copy for *Dramatic Lyrics* in 1842 and needed something to fill up the last two and a half pages (a). RB had written the poem a few months earlier to amuse young Willie Macready, son of the actor-manager, who had been ill in bed with a cough. Willie drew three illustrations to the poem, which he sent to RB (c). Later, when RB's quarrel with Macready over the staging of *A Blot in the 'Scutcheon* became public knowledge, gossips were quick to read significance into lines such as:

> If we've promised them aught, let us keep our promise.

and RB was forced to put the record straight (d):

> It would perhaps have been better to see no "sly hit" in what was merely the obvious moral of a poem meant for a little boy. His father never broke a promise with me nor,—I am sure,—with anybody else. I certainly had a difference with him on quite another matter—but long after the "Pied Piper" was written.

RB was introduced to the Pied Piper legend through books in his father's library. Robert Browning, Sr. wrote his own verse version of the story, which he took from Wanley's *Wonders of the Little World* (b). RB probably learned the essentials from this as well, but used other books, such as Verstegen and Melander (b). Whatever the source, RB's poem is memorable for his imaginative elaboration of the few known facts into a long, vivid narrative—full of humour, pathos and a daring use of rhyme. "The Pied Piper" has been illustrated more than any other Browning work, but one set of illustrations has become synonymous with the poem—that of Kate Greenaway (e). Published in 1889, her representations were admired by RB and have since been reproduced with translations of the poem all over the world.

Men and Women, 1855

86a. Browning, Robert, *Men and Women*, London, 1855

Presentation copy to Alexander Munro, sculptor of Pen's bust (No. 43).

b. Quotations in RB's hand

Seven lines from "Fra Lippo Lippi" copied out for Mrs. Robert Glover, 3 April 1871; and three lines from "Andrea del Sarto" given to the Duke of Sutherland in a copy of *Selections*, 20 December 1884.

c. *Illustrations to Browning's Poems*, with a notice of the artists and the pictures by Ernest Radford, The Browning Society, London, 1882

d. Wilmott, R.A. (ed.), *The Poets of the Nineteenth Century*, London, 1857

"I hope to be listen'd to, this time," wrote RB to John Forster prior to the publication of *Men and Women*, but ten years later copies of the first edition (a) were still unsold. The fifty poems, plus "One Word More" to EBB, are imbued with RB's love for Italy and for Italian Art. The poems reflect his interests and preoccupations during the first few years at Casa Guidi, and demonstrate his mastery of his chosen form, the dramatic monologue. Nowhere is the brilliance of *Men and Women* better shown than in the poems "Fra Lippo Lippi" and "Andrea del Sarto." The manuscript of neither poem survives, but RB occasionally copied out passages for friends (b). The one shown from "Fra Lippo" illustrates the painter-monk's view of art, not dissimilar from RB's own, while that from "Andrea" (mislabelled by RB "Lippo Lippi") captures the tone of Andrea's weary resignation:

I am grown peaceful as old age to-night.
I regret little, I would change still less:
Since there my past life lies, why alter it?

RB used Vasari's *Lives of the Painters* for the backgrounds of both Lippo and Andrea, but a more immediate stimulus was Lippo's "Coronation of the Virgin" and Andrea's "Portrait of the Artist and his Wife," which the Brownings saw in the Florence art galleries. In 1882 the Browning Society issued to its members, in a portfolio, Alinari prints of both paintings with explanatory notes (c).

No illustrated edition of RB's works appeared during his lifetime. While Tennyson enjoyed Moxon's successful 1857 edition of his *Poems*, illustrated by giants of the Pre-Raphaelite movement, RB had to be content with an occasional engraving in an anthology. The first known book illustration of an RB poem is E.A. Goodall's "Two in the Campagna"—from *Men and Women*—which appeared in Wilmott's *Poets of the Nineteenth Century* in 1857 (d).

The Ring and the Book, 1868–1869

87a. Browning, Robert, *The Ring and the Book*, London, 1868–1869, 4 vols.

Presentation copy to Dante Gabriel Rossetti.

b. The Old Yellow Book

Printed texts and manuscripts, vellum-bound; primary source of RB's *The Ring and the Book*.

c. RB's Ring

Gold ring, plain and beaded ribs, rounded bezel with VIS MEA (my strength) in relief. The ring of *The Ring and the Book*.

d. Unsigned review, *The Saturday Review*, 26 December 1868
Letter from John Forster to RB, 18 March 1869

e. Browning, R.W.B., Bust of Pompilia, 1886

Bronze portrait of the heroine of *The Ring and the Book*. (Plate 28)

Do you see this square old yellow Book, I toss
I' the air, and catch again, and twirl about
By the crumpled vellum covers . . . ?
I found this book,
Gave a *lira* for it, eightpence English just . . .
One day still fierce 'mid many a day struck calm,
Across a Square in Florence, crammed with booths,
Buzzing and blaze, noontide and market-time . . .

So RB describes his purchase of the Old Yellow Book (b) from a market-stall outside the church of San Lorenzo in June 1860. The book's 250 pages, nine-tenths in type, the rest in manuscript, give details of the trial of Guido Franceschini, beheaded in Rome in 1698 for the murder of his wife Pompilia and of the poor couple who had brought her up as their child.

The ring (c) is RB's, given to him by Isa Blagden:

> 'Tis Rome-work, made to match
> (By Castellani's imitative craft)
> Etrurian circlets found, some happy morn,
> After a dropping April...

In the first few lines of *The Ring and the Book* RB explains that, just as the workman who made the ring needed an alloy to mix with the gold before he could create the finished masterpiece, so too the poet needs imagination and inspiration before he can turn fact (the information from the Yellow Book) into the poem (*The Ring and the Book*). RB, like the goldsmith, is a workman; and his inspiration is provided by the memory of EBB.

RB planned his Roman murder case for about four years and spent another three years writing it. He consulted at least one secondary source, a pamphlet about the trial, and wrote over 20,000 lines. By 1868 the work was finished; it appeared in four volumes at monthly intervals between November 1868 and February 1869 (a). *The Ring and the Book* is divided into twelve parts. RB is the narrator of the first and last; the rest are dramatic monologues spoken by participants in and witnesses of the main action. In this way the same story is retold from every possible angle: from the murderer, from his dying victim, from the prosecution and defence counsels, from the ordinary citizens of Rome, and from the Pope. Since RB's death, more information has come to light about the Franceschini affair from sources he didn't know. The new facts substantiate the atmosphere he creates in the poem and his analyses of the main characters.

It took time for the poem to be accepted. Early reviews were grudging (d):

> If any one thinks that we have not spoken with due praise of the present poem, let it be remembered that a great poet is judged by a higher standard than other people; nor can any one deny the originality, the compass, and the solidity of Mr. Browning's genius.

but when *The Ring and the Book* was complete, critical opinion was enthusiastic and generous. In a letter to RB, John Forster wrote (d):

> I think it to the very last a very noble performance—sounding greater depths than even you have yet gone to, and wiser with more various kinds of wisdom. I should like to speak in detail of the first and last of the books in this volume ["The Pope" and "The Book and the Ring"]—but, if I began, where should I end—and there are things in both that have so deeply stirred and agitated me that I do not find mere criticism to be just and applicable to them. One thing I will say—that the volume fulfils perfectly your promise of rounding off the Ring. It brings within its circle all that has gone before, and shows that without the soliloquies even of your doctors of law, there would have been a flaw to the completeness. Here is now a Kosmos—a perfected thing ...

The Ring and the Book has retained its initial popularity. In 1886 Pen modelled a bust of Pompilia, which was later cast in bronze (e), depicting the beauty and suffering of the seventeen-year-old mother:

> I looked already old though I was young;
> Do I not ... say, if you are by to speak...
> Look nearer twenty?

88a. Rossetti, D.G., "Hist!"—said Kate the Queen

Oil on canvas, 1851. The subject is taken from a song in *Pippa Passes* (1841) describing the hopeless love of a page-boy for the Queen of Cyprus. It was intended as a sketch for a large picture (4′ x 7½′) which Rossetti abandoned. (Plate 9)

b. Browning, Robert, *Asolando*, London, 1890

Copy given to Fannie Browning by RB on his death-bed. The leather cover was ordered by Fannie, who later presented the book to Wellesley College.

c. RB's draft ms. of "The Cardinal and the Dog"

Written in the margin of p. 611 of RB's copy of Wanley's *Wonders of the Little World*, and dated 27 February 1841.

d. Letter from RB to Mrs. Thomas, 30 May 1889

Enclosing the fair copy of "The Cardinal and the Dog." ("I enclose a little sort of what you may call a childish ballad, hitherto unpublished. Will you offer it for acceptance to the young lady . . .").

RB's final book, published on the day of his death, links the past and the present in an uncanny way. He had discovered the walled hill-town of Asolo on his first Italian journey in 1838. Its beauty and its history appealed to him: particularly the romantic story of the exiled Queen of Cyprus, Caterina Cornaro, who was given Asolo as a compensation for her lost kingdom, and who ruled there from 1489 to 1510. Something of the historical appeal of Asolo can be gleaned from Rossetti's picture illustrating RB's "'Hist!'—said Kate the Queen" from *Pippa Passes* (a). The Queen half-listens to a reading from Boccaccio's *Decamerone* while her maids arrange her hair; outside, her page, hawk on wrist, sings his unrequited love-song to her. Rossetti knew enough about Asolo from RB's poem to introduce silk-makers in the painting; but he had never been to Asolo and so his architecture is fanciful, more like a stage-set than the attractive ruins RB knew. What the canvas captures so well is the colour and lightheartedness of Queen Caterina's court.

Asolo and its Queen haunted RB for the next forty years after his first visit. He returned briefly to the town in 1878, but during the last autumn of his life he stayed there again, as the guest of another Caterina—Katharine Bronson, his American friend who had acquired a house in the town walls. RB had promised Mrs. Bronson that he would write a book to unite their two names. He called it *Asolando*, completing the poems and correcting the proofs in Asolo. An advance copy was sent to Venice and he was able to give it to his daughter-in-law a few hours before he died (b).

Asolando contains some of RB's finest late lyrics, but not all its poems were composed during the last year of his life. For example, "The Cardinal and the Dog," like "The Pied Piper," was written for young Willie Macready, and it remained among RB's papers for nearly fifty years. Like "The Pied Piper," too, it was suggested by Wanley's *Wonders of the Little World* (c). Few of RB's working manuscripts survive, so it is interesting to see the development of "The Cardinal and the Dog" from prose into what RB neatly terms "dog-rel." After many years he was reminded of the poem when he was asked to write something for a little girl in 1889 (d), and he then fitted it into the scheme of *Asolando*. It takes its place as a fanciful memory of childhood in a book which unites youth with age, fancy with fact.

Works of Elizabeth Barrett Browning

"Sonnets from the Portuguese," 1845–1846

89a. Browning, Elizabeth Barrett, "Sonnets from the Portuguese"

Autograph manuscript, printer's copy. Copied by EBB for Chapman and Hall, ca. 1850. This manuscript of 43 sonnets shows a number of variants and corrections when compared with earlier versions in the British Library and the Pierpont Morgan Library.

b. Browning, Elizabeth Barrett, *Poems*, London, 1850, 2 vols. First publication of "Sonnets from the Portuguese"

Chapman and Hall began typesetting *Poems* (1850) while located at 186 Strand. During production, however, they removed to a new address, 193 Piccadilly. The item displayed is, in bibliographical terminology, a very rare copy of the first state of *Poems* (1850)—that is, of the variant which bears only the early address in the publisher's imprint.

c. Browning, Elizabeth Barrett, "Sonnet XLII"

Autograph manuscript, printer's copy, prepared by EBB for Chapman and Hall, ca. 1856.

d. E.B.B., *Sonnets*, Reading, Not for Publication, 1847; ca. 1893 The T.J. Wise Forgery

The "Sonnets from the Portuguese" were secretly written during the Brownings' courtship and given to RB by EBB at Bagni di Lucca in 1849. RB thought the 44 love poems "the finest sonnets written in any language since Shakespeare's" and encouraged his wife to publish them. EBB felt them too personal, and so to preserve anonymity, RB proposed the invention of the Portuguese lady. Why not pretend that they were fictional poems, supposedly written to the great 16th-century Portuguese poet Luis de Camoens by his friend, the dark-haired Donna Catarina Ataide? As EBB had previously written a poem "Catarina to Camoens," the scheme seemed plausible.

EBB tidied the text and prepared fresh manuscripts for her publisher (a) and 43 of the sonnets were printed in the second edition of her collected *Poems* in 1850 (b). One of the original 44 (No. XLII) was omitted at this time because it contained a line which clearly would have identified EBB as the writer, thus destroying the "Catarina" fiction. The telltale sonnet appeared elsewhere, as a separate entry. All this maneuvering was to no avail. The quality of the "Sonnets from the Portuguese" was such that no one was deceived, and EBB had to admit authorship. Thus, the missing sonnet (c) rejoined the others and became No. XLII in *Poems* (1856), replacing "How do I love thee?"—which became No. XLIII.

The truth wasn't enough for the bibliographer T.J. Wise. About 1893 he and his cronies decided to embellish the story by publishing a spurious edition of "Sonnets from the Portuguese" with a false imprint dated 1847 (d). This, they claimed, had been privately printed by Mary Russell Mitford at the Brownings' request after RB had been shown the poems in Pisa in 1847. Indeed one of the forgers, Harry Buxton Forman, changed the story and claimed that EBB had given RB a copy of the forgery itself in Pisa. Luckily the forgery was discovered in the 1930's and the Reading Sonnets remains a bibliographical curiosity.

On display, in addition to the wandering No. XLII, is the next-to-final poem of the sequence, popularly known today as the 43rd Sonnet.

How do I love thee? Let me count the ways–
I love thee to the depth and breadth and height
My soul can reach, when feeling out of sight
For the ends of Being and Ideal Grace.
I love thee to the level of everyday's
Most quiet need, by sun and candlelight–
I love thee freely, as men strive for Right;
I love thee purely, as they turn from Praise:
I love thee with the passion put to use
In my old griefs, and with my childhood's faith:
I love thee with a love I seemed to lose
With my lost saints! I love thee with the breath,
Smiles, tears, of all my life!—and, if God choose,
I shall but love thee better after death–

Aurora Leigh, 1857

90a. Browning, Elizabeth Barrett, *Aurora Leigh*, London, 1857

b. Browning, Elizabeth Barrett, *Aurora Leigh*, New York, 1857

Susan B. Anthony's copy of the first American edition.

c. Notebook

Presented to EBB by Arabella Moulton-Barrett, containing the first draft of *Aurora Leigh*, 353 pp.

d. Rossetti, Dante Gabriel, Pencil correction to portrait of EBB

Pencil notes correcting a proof of an engraving of EBB by T.O. Barlow.

e. Browning, Elizabeth Barrett, *Aurora Leigh*, fourth edition, London, 1859

The first revised edition, and the first to have the engraved portrait.

EBB's novel in verse, intended to deal unflinchingly with "the aspect and manners of modern life," succeeded beyond her greatest hopes. The first edition (a) sold out in two weeks. *Aurora Leigh* then went through twenty-two editions in thirty years, attracting the praise of Rossetti, Swinburne and Ruskin. EBB had planned the outline of the story ten years before, but wrote the bulk of the poem between 1853 and 1856. *Aurora Leigh* was sketched out in a notebook (c) which EBB carried with her to Paris, London and the Isle of Wight, almost losing it on one occasion among some missing luggage. Originally she called her heroine Aurora Vane, but by the time she showed her husband the poem ("Read this Book, this divine Book, Wednesday night, July 9th, '56.—R.B.") she had changed the name to Leigh.

The poem, championing as it does the cause of women's independence, was as important in its day as Ibsen's *A Doll's House*:

The honest earnest man must stand and work.
The woman also,—otherwise she drops
At once below the dignity of man
Accepting serfdom. Free men freely work.

For this reason it was Susan B. Anthony's favourite book. When she presented her copy to the Library of Congress, she wrote in it (b): "This book was carried in my satchel for years and read & re-read. The noble words of Elizabeth Barrett—as Wendell Phillips always called her—sink deep into my heart. . . . With the hope that Women may more & more be like 'Aurora Leigh'." It would, however, be a pity if *Aurora Leigh* were seen only as a tract. The descriptions of the English and Italian countryside, some of the crowd scenes and much of the dialogue read well today, even though the plot and some of the characterization more resemble an opera than a realistic novel.

Contemporary demand for the work was so great that EBB's publishers suggested an engraving of the author as a frontispiece to the fourth edition in 1859 (e). EBB provided one of the photographs taken the year before at Le Havre, but the engraver, T.O. Barlow, had difficulty and needed the help of Dante Gabriel Rossetti, who knew EBB well, to get the image right (d). The proof, with Rossetti's suggestions, makes an interesting comment on EBB's appearance:

> The mouth is considerably in need of correction. This may be done by adding a line of shadow all along the top of the upper lip, thus lessening the curve upward at the corner which gives a sort of smile not in the photograph & not characteristic of the original.

Poems Before Congress, 1860

91a. Browning, Elizabeth Barrett, *Poems Before Congress*, London, 1860

Henrietta Cook's copy inscribed in her hand "From her dearest Ba—the Authoress March 24th 1860."

b. Another copy

Inscribed by EBB: "William C Cartwright deprecatingly & with kindest regards from the author– Rome– 1860." This modest inscription may anticipate Cartwright's possible dislike of the book, as he failed to share EBB's enthusiasm for Napoleon III.

c. Browning, Elizabeth Barrett, *Napoleon III In Italy*, New York, 1860

Inscribed by EBB and containing her autograph corrections to the Preface.

d. Photograph of Cavour

EBB's copy, from her album of political and literary portraits.

e. Giuseppe Mazzini, Address supporting the Italian Cause

Document in Mazzini's hand encouraging Englishmen to join the call for Italian Unity.

Poems Before Congress demonstrates EBB's passionate support for Italian unity—"a thin slice of a wicked book," intended to shame Englishmen out of their complacency towards a struggle which had been going on since 1830. In it are expressed her admiration for Napoleon III, her dislike of Austria and her distrust of the Pope. Although EBB believed in the sentiments of Mazzini (e):

> The aim . . . of the Italian struggle . . . is *Nationality*: the "to be or not to be" of Hamlet: the want of one Italy from the Alps to the Sicilian Sea; the

> feeling that the 25 millions of people between those limits, are millions of brothers, called by God and the general will to live under the same compact, under the same political laws, with the same rights to exercise, with the same duties to fulfil, under a common flag and a common name.

she was to the centre-right of the Italian revolution, supporting Napoleon and Cavour rather than Garibaldi. Above all she put her hope for the future in Cavour, whose portrait she placed in her photographic album (d):

> Robert brought me in, one of the new photograph-books . . books to receive photographs—crimson leather, clasped in gold, with so many prepared frames in card, into which you slip the photographs– Mine holds a hundred– I had been longing for one, as I want to make a collection of the portraits of all the public men mixed up with the Italian question– These photographs seem to me the most deeply interesting possible sights—the very faces of the men . . & their souls—as far as souls are seen in faces. Robert brought me, too, a heap of photographs to begin my collection. Was'nt it kind? I told him I would rather have it than . . . . "*diamonds*," I said . . & that was poor praise.

The thin red book (a) created a stir when it was published in England. The poems were too strident—mediocre vehicles for the strong feelings EBB expressed in them. The final poem, "A Curse for a Nation" was completely misunderstood. Taken by some critics to be a condemnation of England's non-intervention in Italian affairs, it was intended to be a criticism of slavery in America. The more sober American edition (c) was better received and better understood, but *Poems Before Congress* is more interesting today for its politics than its poetry. EBB was tiring when she wrote it, and it was to be the last book she published.

THEIR FRIENDS

HUGH STUART BOYD (1781–1848)

A Greek scholar with a daughter of Elizabeth's age, H.S. Boyd came to live at Ruby Cottage near Hope End in 1825 when Elizabeth was nineteen. It took them two years to get acquainted and a further year before they met, but the blind Mr. Boyd eventually became a close friend to Elizabeth, fulfilling her need for challenging intellectual company. They corresponded regularly and studied Greek texts together—not merely the tragedians but also the early Greek Church Fathers. When the Barretts moved to Sidmouth in August 1832, Mr. Boyd followed them in December, after which he and Elizabeth spent another year studying together. By now, however, she was beginning to find his scholarship pedantic and his set ways trying; so their friendship cooled but never broke. In the mid-1830's Boyd went to London, as did the Barretts, and contacts continued there. After Elizabeth's marriage, in 1846, she wrote to Boyd from Pisa: "Looking back through all these thick vapours of dreamland, to the friends whom I best love in England, your name stands among the very first."

92. [Barrett, E.B.], *Prometheus Bound, and Other Poems*, London, 1833

Inscribed "To H.S. Boyd Esqr. from his affectionate friend Elizabeth B. Barrett." Elizabeth's translation of Æschylus's *Prometheus* was published in May, so presumably she gave this copy to Boyd during one of their meetings in Sidmouth. The previous year she had sought Boyd's advice about the wisdom of allowing her father to have the translation published. With Boyd, EBB had read all the works of Æschylus, Boyd's favourite playwright.

93. Sophocles, *Tragoediae Septem*, Oxford, 1820

EBB's copy. She had read Sophocles with Boyd between July and November 1830, and it was then that she embellished this copy with hundreds of notes and comments. At times she is almost having a dialogue with herself, as on the page of the *Philoctetes* shown:

> November 6th 1830. This play has affected and interested me very much. It is exquisitely beautiful. Is it not more distinguished for *delineation of character* than any play of Sophocles?

94. Browning, E.B., Autograph ms., "Hugh Stuart Boyd. His Death, 1848"

EBB was in Florence when she heard of Boyd's death. She interrupted work on *Casa Guidi Windows* to write three sonnets which were first published in the 1850 edition of her *Poems*. In the second Boyd is described as Elizabeth's:

> Stedfast friend,
> Who never didst, my heart or life, misknow,
> Nor either's faults, too keenly apprehend...

Mary Russell Mitford (1787–1855)

As her friendship with Boyd waned, EBB found a new friend in the popular author of *Our Village*, Mary Russell Mitford, almost twenty years her senior. They were introduced by John Kenyon on 27 May 1836 and spent that afternoon together at the London Zoo. This meeting resulted in a vivid correspondence which was to last until Miss Mitford's death and lead to the exchange of nearly five hundred letters from each correspondent. Elizabeth reveals herself as a most vivid letter-writer, and she quickly changes from Miss Mitford's protegée to her literary equal. Soon after their meeting she was contributing poems to annuals edited by Miss Mitford. After the shock which EBB suffered upon the death of her brother, "Bro," in 1840, Miss Mitford gave her the dog Flush (named for her own spaniel) as a comfort. Then Elizabeth provided much-needed moral support during the lingering final illness of Miss Mitford's father, Dr. George Mitford. The two seldom met, but their friendship survived Elizabeth's marriage and Miss Mitford's indiscreet publication of details about Bro's death. Miss Mitford also knew Browning, thought him effeminate and unworthy, but gradually became reconciled to the marriage.

95. Three letters from EBB to Miss Mitford, [19 February 1844], [10 August 1844], [31 October 1844]

These three notes written during 1844 are uncharacteristic of the long, news-filled letters EBB usually wrote to her friend. They do, however, show EBB's spontaneity and how the mood of the moment dictated her feelings in the sickroom at Wimpole Street. In the first she is "nearly worn out with the weather—weak & weary—& it is an effort to take pleasure .. as in writing to *you* ... If such weather lasted, life wd. scarcely be worth the trouble, even with Balzac under the pillow." Later in the year she is ebullient: "I shall be delighted, delighted, delighted, to a three times three, or nine times nine of repetitions, to see you on Saturday."

96. Mitford, Mary Russell, *Recollections of a Literary Life*, London, 1852, 3 vols.

This series of essays was very popular. The Brownings are given a chapter called "Married Poets" in Vol. 1; it is here that the passage about Bro's drowning occurs. EBB remonstrated with Miss Mitford: I have been miserably upset by your book . . . if I had had the least imagination of your intending to touch upon certain biographical details in relation to me, I would have conjured you by your love to me & by my love to you to forbear it altogether."

97. Mitford, Mary Russell, Letter to EBB, [2 October 1847]

A good example of the continuing literary commentary that played a large part in the exchange of letters between Miss Mitford and EBB. Discussing Lamartine's *Histoire des Girondins*, Miss Mitford says: "Do read that. Even at the Palace where they read so little they are all devouring those eloquent Volumes—the Queen & all."

JOHN KENYON, (1784–1856)

John Kenyon, who introduced Elizabeth to Miss Mitford, was later to be even more influential in her life by introducing her to Robert Browning. A rich distant cousin of the Moulton-Barretts, Kenyon published poetry, dabbled in the Arts and was one of the few regular visitors to Wimpole Street. He greatly admired Elizabeth's poetry and listened to her praise of Browning's work. Having been at school with Browning's father, he knew Robert and encouraged the two to meet. When she refused, he urged Browning to write to her, and so the famous correspondence started. After the marriage, the Brownings kept closely in touch with Kenyon, visiting him on the Isle of Wight just before his death in 1856. Elizabeth dedicated *Aurora Leigh* to him. In his will John Kenyon left the Brownings £11,000.

98. Moulton-Barrett, Alfred, Portrait of John Kenyon

This sketch, made during 1843 when Alfred was drawing members of his family and the household, shows that Kenyon was accepted as part of the Wimpole Street menage at this time.

99. [Barrett, E.B.], *An Essay on Mind, with Other Poems*, London, 1826

A remarkable copy of EBB's second book. Brought to Torquay by her father and given there to Kenyon, it was later given by Kenyon to RB on 10 December 1845. By this time RB was visiting Wimpole Street regularly and had fallen deeply in love with Elizabeth.

100. Letter from John Kenyon to Mrs. Adey, 7 March 1846

This letter discusses the works and characters of RB and EBB a year before their elopement:

> I warned you about Browning—still you will think me a little cracked or blinded by his liking for me– But you will *more* than like Miss B . . . and *she* thinks B. the very first of all our poets—and (like Landor) would put

him on a level with Chaucer. But to measure the depth & power of EBB—you must read her over and over again– Deep thoughts and feelings are not to be skimmed—nor are they accepted in every mood of one's own mind.

101. Kenyon, John, *A Day At Tivoli*, London, 1849

Copy of Kenyon's last book. It bears a dedication to the Brownings: "This poem, referring to the land which they now inhabit, is affectionately inscribed."

Euphrasia Fanny Haworth, (1801–1883)

Fanny Haworth runs like a thread through Browning's life. She lived at Elstree near W.C. Macready, at whose house they first met. Fanny Haworth admired Browning's early poetry, particularly *Paracelsus*, and later enjoyed *Sordello*, in which she makes a brief appearance as the "English Eyebright." Browning wrote her bubbling letters about his works and hopes. These ceased with his marriage, but Fanny Haworth (with her friend Ellen Heaton) came to Florence, where she became a friend of Elizabeth and of Isa Blagden. A talented amateur artist, Miss Haworth painted three pictures of Pen (see No. 51a) and made a drawing of Sarianna. She later lived at Versailles, where Browning visited her in the 1860's; she also joined Robert and Sarianna on one of their holidays in France. Browning always had great respect for her judgment, and sent her presentation copies of his poems.

102a. Letter from RB to E.F. Haworth, [1 July 1837]

"I firmly believe you wrote those Sonnets—don't ask me why. At all events I wish you to have written them; and am sure you did."

b. Haworth, Euphrasia Fanny. "On the Author of Paracelsus"

Copies in the hand of W.C. Macready of Miss Haworth's two sonnets; the first reads as follows:

Thy brow is calm, young Poet—pale and clear
  As a moonlighted statue. I might deem,
I but behold thy pictured semblance near,—
  And yet I did behold thee in no dream!
Unmoved, unheeding as thine eyes appear,
  Quick and shaded like an unsunned stream.

  Those very eyes may often flash and beam
With thought intense, or melt in feeling's tear,
  As genius lights them with a ray divine.
Methinks, when in deep solitude I pore
Over the wonders of thy mind's rich store,
  That I am glad, thou didst not smile and speak
  With common smiles and words, and rudely break
The Poet's image in my Fancy's shrine.

103. Letter from Edmund Gosse to W.B. Douglas, 18 December 1881

"Mr. Browning tells me that the English Eyebright of the 3rd book of *Sordello* was a private friend of his, Miss Euphrasia Haworth, who still survives at a great age."

ALFRED DOMETT, (1811–1887)

The poet and colonial administrator Alfred Domett was an early friend from Camberwell, a member of the literary circle, "The Colloquials," which RB was invited to join. He and Browning were intimates between 1840 and 1842, Browning feeling for him a "real love ... better love than I had supposed I was fit for." Browning admired Domett's intellectual powers, while Domett gave Browning great support and encouragement after the failure of *Sordello*. In 1842 Domett left England to take up a new life in New Zealand. Browning wrote a number of poems in which he referred to his friend, including "Waring" and "Popularity," and corresponded with him until 1846. Their friendship resumed in 1871, when Domett returned from New Zealand to live in London. Browning never forgot those few friends who had stood by his early writing, and Domett was always a welcome visitor to Warwick Crescent.

104. Letter from RB to Alfred Domett, 19 December 1841

A characteristic letter, showing RB's affection for his friend:

> It is surely a long time since we foregathered. What say you to coming here next Wednesday?– Our little hills are stiff & springy underfoot with the frozen grass—and you crunch the thin-white ice on the holes the cattle have made—hedge & tree are glazed bright with rime—(to speak Bucolically)– *Do* disappoint all other lovers of good-company and promise me to run over not later than 2. o'Clock. Last week I spent an evening with Carlyle and the next morning with Landor– "What are all these seeings worth, If thou &c &c"

105. Browning, Robert, "Waring" in *Dramatic Lyrics*, November 1842

Written after Domett's departure for New Zealand, "Waring" is "a fancy portrait of a very dear friend":

> What's become of Waring
> Since he gave us all the slip,
> Chose land-travel or seafaring,
> Boots and chest or staff and scrip,
> Rather than pace up and down
> Any longer London town?

106. Domett, Alfred, *Flotsam and Jetsam*, London, 1871

RB's copy. A collection of poems dedicated to RB ("A mighty poet and a subtle-souled psychologist"), it includes "Lines sent to Robert Browning, 1840, on a certain critique on 'Pippa Passes'":

> A black squat Beetle, potent for his size,
> Pushing tail-first by every road that's wrong,
> The dirt-ball of his musty rules along–
> His tiny sphere of grovelling sympathies,–
> Has knocked himself full-butt with blundering trouble
> Against a Mountain...

107. Browning, Robert, *Dramatic Idyls*, London, 1879

Inscribed by RB: "Alfred Domett with his old friend & admirer's affectionate regards. Apr. 26. '79." This copy contains a pencil sketch said to be of a youthful RB.

Richard Henry Horne, (1803–1884)

The eccentric poet Richard Henry (later "Hengist") Horne became one of Elizabeth's most persistent correspondents during her seclusion in Wimpole Street. Horne, who sold his epic *Orion* at the cost of a farthing a copy to promote the cause of poetry, persuaded Elizabeth to collaborate in two ventures with him—a modern version of Chaucer (1841) and a collection of essays on contemporary literary figures, *A New Spirit of the Age* (1844). When the latter was published, Horne presented her with a set of the engravings used as illustrations, including one of Browning. For Horne, Elizabeth was the ideal collaborator—one "who has magnanimity to admire, as well as moral courage to demur or denounce, ever holding within, as at a shrine, an unmixed love and spirit of truth. Such a friend and counsellor ... I had in Miss Barrett." They did not meet until 1851. Horne had, however, met Browning. They were often at the same literary supper parties in the late 1830's, but were never particularly friendly. Horne, like Domett, left England for the Southern Hemisphere; in 1852 he went to prospect for gold in Australia. On his return, he sought Browning's permission to publish the letters Elizabeth had written him between 1839 and 1851. Rather surprisingly, Browning agreed (1877). In the last years of his life Horne fell upon ill days and Browning supported a petition which gave him a Civil Pension.

108. Horne, R.H., *A New Spirit of the Age*, London, 1844

Elizabeth contributed the essays on Wordsworth, Leigh Hunt, Carlyle and Landor; she also made numerous suggestions, most of which Horne adopted. She was not shown the manuscript or proof of Horne's essay about her, and was displeased at the inaccuracy of some of the biographical information.

109. Letter from EBB to R.H. Horne, 5 March 1844

"You are guilty of certain exaggerations ... I have not been 'shut up in one room for six or seven years'—four or five wd. be nearer; & then, except on one occasion, I have not been for 'several weeks together in the dark,' during the course of them." Horne changed the offending passages in time for the second edition.

110. Engraving of RB by J.C. Armytage

This engraving appeared in Vol. II of *A New Spirit of the Age* to illustrate the article about Browning and J.W. Marston. EBB framed the copy Horne gave her; but, after she had met Browning, declared it "a vulgarized caricature":

> Speaking of the portrait of you in the 'Spirit of the Age' .. which is not like .. no!—which has not your character, in a line of it .. something in just the forehead & eyes & hair .. but even *that*, thrown utterly out of your order, by another bearing so unlike you!

Isa Blagden (1817–1873)

Isa Blagden—"perfect in friendship"—was the Brownings' closest friend during their time in Florence. A tiny, dark-haired, Eurasian woman of great vivacity and sympathy, Isa arrived in Florence at about the same time as did the poets. For

the next twenty years she lived in rented villas at and near Bellosguardo. The most famous of these—Villa Bricchieri—became the focus of the Anglo-Florentine community and was described in *Aurora Leigh*. Isa and Elizabeth had much in common: their interest in spiritualism was matched by their interest in literature and in people. "You are an angel, dearest Isa," wrote Elizabeth, "with the tact of a woman of the world." When Elizabeth died, Isa took Pen back to her house and then looked after Robert during a traumatic month. She spent the next year in London, during which time she visited Browning often. When she returned to Florence, they corresponded regularly every month—she writing on the 12th and he on the 19th. Their deep friendship, revealed in his intimate letters, was founded on an implied understanding of what Elizabeth had meant to each of them. "No human being can give me one hand—with the feeling on my part that the other holds that of my own Ba—as you can and do," he declared. When Isa Blagden died she was buried a few yards away from Elizabeth in the Protestant Cemetery in Florence.

111. Blagden, I., *Agnes Tremorne*, London, 1861

Isa wrote five novels, *Agnes Tremorne* being the first. A sentimental romance set in Rome during the Risorgimento, its "good high feeling" appealed to RB. "I see *you* in it all, what you approve, what you disapprove, and entirely agree with you," he wrote. Isa used a quotation from RB's "A Serenade at the Villa" on the title-page. There are other Browning details in the story itself, such as the Etruscan ring which Imogene drew from Herbert's finger and which was identical with one Isa gave RB.

112. Blagden, Isa, *Poems*, London, 1873

This posthumous collection of Isa's poems was edited by Alfred Austin, much to RB's disgust. Several of the poems contain unexpected delights and show Isa to have been a good lyricist.

113. Letter from RB to Isa Blagden, 25 June 1861

Written during EBB's last illness, four days before she died:

> Ba is better but still very weak & incapable of talking or being talked to—& who can look at your face without being tempted to the one, or expecting the other?

Eliza Ogilvy (1822–1912)

The Brownings knew most of the Anglo-Florentine community. Their nearest neighbours were David and Eliza Ogilvy, who for a time rented an apartment two floors above them in Casa Guidi. The Ogilvys' son, Alexander, was exactly the same age as Pen, and Mrs. Ogilvy wrote poetry. The two families went to Venice together in 1851 and the following year visited Paris. Although EBB and Mrs. Ogilvy had much in common, EBB found the Scottish lady a little stern—"a want of softness in the character .. a want of tenderness." She was "agreeable": a woman to like rather than to love.

114. Browning, Elizabeth Barrett, *Last Poems*, London, 1862

Inscribed "A. & E. Ogilvy with RB's kindest regard London. May 11. '62." There is no evidence to suggest that RB kept in touch with the

Ogilvys after EBB's death, probably because he and David Ogilvy had few common interests.

115. Ogilvy, Eliza A.H., Recollections, Ms., ca. 1857

In 1893 Mrs. Ogilvy was asked to contribute an introduction to an edition of EBB's poems. She had already written a brief memoir of her meeting and friendship with the Brownings in her commonplace book during the late 1850's. She drew heavily on this for the introduction. The passage displayed from the original manuscript describes Mrs. Ogilvy's first impressions of EBB:

> She was just like a King Charles Spaniel, the same large soft brown eyes, the full silky curls falling round her face like a spaniel's ears, the same pathetic wistfulness of expression. Her mouth was too large for beauty, but full of eloquent curves and movements. Her voice was very expressive, her manner gentle but full of energy. At times she became intense in tone and gesture, but it was so spontaneous, that nobody could ever have thought it assumed.

JOSEPH MILSAND (1817–1886)

"No words can express the love I have for him, you know—he is increasingly precious to me," wrote Browning in 1872 to Isa Blagden about Joseph Milsand. This French critic and philosopher first met Browning in Paris in 1852, after publishing an article in *La Revue des Deux Mondes* praising the latter's early work. They never lost contact. Milsand used to stay at Warwick Crescent for a month every Spring; Browning and Sarianna made sure they visited Milsand whenever they were in France. On several occasions they all spent holidays together at St. Aubin, where Milsand owned a small cottage. In 1865 Milsand married (once his mother's death had removed family opposition), but his friendship with Browning remained unbroken. Browning was warm in his praise for Milsand, whom he called "my own heart's man-friend." He describes him in *Red Cotton Night-Cap Country*:

> He knows more and loves better than the world
> That never heard his name and never may...
> O friend! who makest warm my wintry world,
> And wise my heaven, if there we consort too.

Browning dedicated the revision of *Sordello* to Milsand in 1863, and *Parleyings with Certain People of Importance* (1887) was dedicated to his memory. For his part, Milsand was a loyal friend to Robert and Sarianna and a great advocate of Browning's genius.

116. Robert Browning and Joseph Milsand, 1884

Photograph sent by RB to Mrs. Bronson. RB and Milsand are looking at one of Pen's portraits during Milsand's annual month in London.

117. Letter from Joseph Milsand to Sarianna Browning, 20 October 1877

This letter concerns a dispute between RB and Pen, which Milsand has been asked to mediate. Milsand explains that he has contacted Pen in Paris and tried to make him see sense about the need to work harder and not to distress his father. He hopes that Robert and Sarianna will understand that he couldn't proceed further. The letter suggests that the cause of friction between RB and his son was a promise Pen had made to a girl; which Milsand did not feel qualified to deal with. The letter shows how closely Milsand was involved in Browning's personal family affairs, and also the high regard in which he held Sarianna. She spent holidays in France with M. and Mme. Milsand when RB was elsewhere.

118. *Revue Contemporaine*, Vol. 27, Paris, 15 September 1856

Contains Milsand's 30-page review of *Men and Women*. RB's copy, sent to him by the author, who has added numerous corrections.

ALFRED TENNYSON (1809–1892)

Elizabeth was a great admirer of Tennyson as poet and as man. Browning maintained a more ambiguous attitude towards the Poet Laureate. On the surface the two men were friendly, even generous to one another, but there were times when Tennyson's popularity and large sales rankled. Browning refused all invitations to visit Tennyson at Freshwater, perhaps sensing that Tennyson had a low opinion of his poetry. Browning had great respect for Tennyson's work and was quick to stifle any suggestion of rivalry between the two poets. They met from time to time in London, and Browning was godfather to one of Tennyson's grandchildren.

119. Browning, Robert, *A Selection from the Works*, London, 1865

Dedication copy, presented to Tennyson, 10 October 1865. RB had been invited by Moxon to prepare a second selection of his poems only two years after Chapman and Hall had published a first selection. Not wishing to duplicate material, RB chose completely different poems, revised the text, and dedicated the book to Tennyson, whose illustrated *Poems* Moxon had published in 1857. It is to this work of Tennyson that RB refers when he states in his introduction that his poems look "pale beside the wonderful flower-show of my illustrious predecessor—dare I say? my dear friend: who will take it, all except the love in the gift, at a mere nosegay's worth."

120a. Tennyson, Alfred, *Maud, and other Poems*, London, 1855

Inscribed by Tennyson: "Robert & Elizabeth Barrett Browning from A Tennyson." RB has added: "Thursday, September 27. 13 Dorset St. Manchester Sq."

b. Rossetti, Dante Gabriel, "Tennyson Reading *Maud*"

Ink and sepia wash, inscribed by Rossetti, presented to the Brownings.

In late September 1855 the Brownings were staying in London when Tennyson came up from the Isle of Wight for a few days. EBB described how he "spent two of them with us, dined with us, smoked with us, opened his heart to us (and the second bottle of port), and ended by reading *Maud* through from end to end, and going away at half-past two in the morning. If I had had a heart to spare, certainly he would have won mine." She was entranced. "He is captivating with his frankness, confidingness and unexampled *naivete*! Think of his stopping in *Maud* every now and then—'There's a wonderful touch! That's very tender. How beautiful that is!' Yes, and it *was* wonderful, tender, beautiful, and he read exquisitely in a voice like an organ, rather music than speech." When Tennyson had finished RB replied by reading "Fra Lippo Lippi." Rossetti was also present and, unknown to Tennyson, celebrated the occasion by drawing the sketch on display. (Plate 22)

FREDERIC LEIGHTON (1830–1896)

Among contemporary painters D.G. Rossetti was Browning's most enthusiastic supporter, but Rossetti was not a comfortable person to know. Browning preferred the more conventional Frederic Leighton. Their friendship was grounded in mutual admiration of each other's work. Meeting first in Rome, when Leighton was in his twenties, they soon became easy and affectionate friends. Leighton made a pencil sketch of Browning in 1859, and later designed Elizabeth's tomb (see No. 56). During the last thirty years of Browning's life, they saw each other regularly and Browning elicited Leighton's support in furthering Pen's artistic career. Leighton was a pall-bearer at Browning's funeral.

121. Browning, Robert, *Jocoseria*, London, 1883

Presentation copy: "Sir Frederick Leighton from his old friend RB. March 9. '83." RB always misspelled Leighton's first name.

122a. Browning, Robert, *Balaustion's Adventure*, London, 1871

Dedication copy presented to Countess Cowper.

b. Photograph of Frederic Leighton's painting "Hercules wrestling with Death for the Body of Alcestis"

RB wrote *Balaustion's Adventure* in four weeks to please Lady Cowper, "a May-month amusement" he tells her in the dedication. She had asked him playfully the previous year to be her bard and translate something of Euripides for her. RB remembered this when he visited Leighton's studio and saw him working on his "Hercules wrestling with Death for the Body of Alcestis," which was exhibited at the Royal Academy in the Spring of 1871, and he decided to translate Euripides' *Alcestis* for Lady Cowper, setting it in a framework of his own. In the poem Balaustion anachronistically refers to Leighton's picture in a passage beginning:

> I know, too, a great Kaunian painter, strong
> As Heracles, though rosy with a robe
> Of grace that softens down the sinewy strength:
> And he has made a picture of it all.

Leighton was touched by this 25-line tribute: "I know the value of the pen which has painted over again, and better in repainting, my insufficient work—and of the page in which you have given it a lasting home and an added dignity."

123. Letter from RB to Frederic Leighton, 18 January 1865

Leighton remained a bachelor, deeply attached to his parents. His mother died in January 1865 and RB wrote:

> You very well know how much I love you and that a joy or a sorrow to you must be felt by myself also in the due degree. You will bear up like the good, brave fellow you are, against this loss, irreparable as it is: and I am

sure of one thing,—though you may hardly be able to see it yet,—that to pass away in a fit season, surrounded by the devotedness of such children as your Mother's, is indeed a blessing among the chances of this world.

William Wetmore Story (1819–1895)

Browning's forty-year friendship with the American sculptor William Wetmore Story was more than a meeting of compatible personalities and like minds. In the early years of their acquaintance Browning spent three hours a day in Story's studio; Story, in his turn, wrote Browningesque monologues. Each gave practical help to the other: each sampled the other's craft. They met in Florence in 1848, and the two families became closely allied in 1853, when they both spent the summer at Bagni di Lucca. In Rome and Siena between 1859 and 1861 they saw one another daily and Pen grew to like the Storys' daughter, Edith, four years older than he. It was at this time that Story modelled Browning's head (No. 32a). After Elizabeth's death, Story was desolate when Browning returned to London. "I have lost my best friend and daily companion in Italy. There is no one to take his place," he wrote. Later he saw Browning once a year on visits to England and the two men renewed acquaintance during Browning's visits to Italy in the 1880's. Edith Story, who married the Italian Marchese Peruzzi, remained on close terms with Pen; after the death of her husband and the desertion by Fannie, she cheered her childhood friend's last years with her kindness and support.

124. Browning, Elizabeth Barrett, *Aurora Leigh*, fourth edition, London, 1859

Inscribed by EBB to the Storys during the period of strongest friendship between the two families.

125. Browning, Robert, *Prince Hohenstiel-Schwangau*, London, 1871

Presented to Edith Story in London in 1871.

126. Story, W.W., *Graffiti D'Italia*, New York, 1868

Story published several books of poetry, but *Graffiti D'Italia* is the one most influenced by RB. Many of the poems have Renaissance, Italian or artistic settings and are in the form of monologues. "Praxiteles and Phryne," dedicated to RB, may owe something to the second part of "Pippa Passes."

Benjamin Jowett (1817–1893)

Browning's love of the Classics and of classical scholarship was nurtured during the last thirty years of his life by Benjamin Jowett, who, in 1870, became Master of Balliol College, Oxford. Browning had corresponded with Jowett as early as 1865 about prospects of Pen's going to Balliol. Jowett encouraged the boy to work towards passing the examinations, but in 1868—the year Jowett obtained the offer of an honorary M.A. for Browning—Pen gave up the struggle for entry to academic Balliol and chose social Christ Church instead. Browning was granted rooms in Balliol and always stayed there during visits to Oxford. The two men respected each other's intellect and progressive drive, but Jowett was not an admirer of Browning's later poetry. Jowett welcomed Pen's portrait of his father, which Browning presented to Balliol in 1886.

127. Browning, Robert, *Aristophanes' Apology*, London, 1875

Presentation copy to Jowett—"The Master of Balliol from his friend Robert Browning. Apr. 23, '75." Jowett started reading this book, which contains a translation of Euripides' *Hercules Furens*, but didn't complete it.

128. Letter from Jowett to RB, 18 August 1885

Jowett reminds RB that he had promised to give Balliol the portrait which at the time was being exhibited in London. RB had offered the painting in May, but the proud father showed it to so many friends and fellow-artists that it didn't reach Balliol until March 1886. It was hung in the Dining Hall and is now in the Balliol College Library.

Annie Egerton Smith (d. 1877)

Had it not been for her sudden death, on holiday with Browning and his sister in 1877, Annie Egerton Smith's friendship with Browning would have been forgotten. Today it stands commemorated in his poem, *La Saisiaz*, dedicated to her. Miss Egerton Smith was a lady of independent means, part owner of the *Liverpool Mercury* newspaper, who lived in London. She shared Browning's musical tastes and they regularly went to concerts together. In 1874–77 she joined Browning and Sarianna on holidays in France, and it was on the last of these that she died suddenly of a heart attack in Villa La Saisiaz at the foot of the Salève, five miles SW. of Geneva. During his thirty years as a widower, Browning had a number of women friends, all of whom he treated with the same warmth and generosity. They were all cultured and intelligent—among them Mrs. Benson, Miss Wedgwood and Mrs. FitzGerald—and fulfilled a genuine need he had for companionship. Among these, Annie Egerton Smith was no doubt socially the easiest. At her death she was slowly taking the place Isa Blagden had formerly possessed.

129a. Browning, Robert, *Pacchiarotto*, London, 1876

b. Browning, Robert, *Poetical Works*, London, 1865

Presentation copies to Annie Egerton Smith, the second given to her on holiday in 1867 at Croisic.

130. Browning, Robert, *La Saisiaz*, and *The Two Poets of Croisic*, London, 1878

Presentation copy to A.C. Swinburne. *La Saisiaz*, which is dedicated to Miss Egerton Smith, starts with a description of the climb up the Salève which RB made on the day after her death, and which they were to have done together:

> Dared and done: at last I stand upon the summit, Dear and True!
> Singly dared and done; the climbing both of us were bound to do.
> Petty feat and yet prodigious: every side my glance was bent
> O'er the grandeur and the beauty lavished through the whole ascent.

131. The New Testament

Given to EBB by her sister Arabella. It contains an English prose version of lines from Dante used by RB in *La Saisiaz*:

> "Thus I believe, thus I affirm, thus I am certain, and that from this life I shall pass to another better, there, where that Lady lives, of whom my soul was enamoured." RB. July 31. 1862.

KATHARINE BRONSON (1834–1901)

Katharine Bronson, American expatriate living on the Grand Canal in Venice, became one of Browning's closest friends in the 1880's. Emotionally she took the place vacated by Isa Blagden and Annie Egerton Smith, and on two occasions almost became even closer. The second of these was in Asolo during the last autumn of Browning's life. Mrs. Bronson had entertained him several times at Ca' Alvisi in Venice in previous years—but Asolo was different. This was Browning's special city. Memories of his visit there in 1838, of Pippa, of Elizabeth, came together as he wrote and arranged his final book of poems—which he dedicated to Mrs. Bronson. He tried, unsuccessfully, to tell her how much she meant to him in the "Epilogue" to *Asolando* and in "Inapprehensiveness." But her role in his life remained that of the friend—the "more than friend"—who helped him summarize his life's work in his poetry during his final six years.

132a. Bronson, Katharine, Draft ms. of verse to RB, 1 November 1881:

> Prince of word painters, I dare offer thee
> Venetian shadows, colourless and drear—
> Since the fair dial of thy memory
> Has only marked the sunshine of the year
> And can recall with a magician's skill
> Its own dear Venice, at its own dear will.

b. Browning, Robert, Ms., verse to Katharine Bronson, 4 November 1883:

> K. DE K. BRONSON
>
> Pray, do I write your name the proper way?
> Dear Friend, I think so: and yet, sooth to say,
> I see one striking error: come what may,
> My love for you admits of no D.K.!

133. Browning, Robert, Manuscripts of "Helen's Tower" and "Sonnet to Rawdon Brown"
Given by RB to Katharine Bronson

134. Bound book of letters from RB to Katharine Bronson

After RB's death Mrs. Bronson and her friend Zina Hulton assembled all RB's letters and had them mounted into this memorial book. It is open at a letter dated 16 September 1884:

> The end of the journey was at the Venice Station when the first blessing was that of Luigi's fat face—lighting the way a few footsteps farther to the more than Friend who had come in the rain to take us and keep us.

ALEXANDRA SUTHERLAND ORR (1828–1903)
JOHN T. NETTLESHIP (1841–1902)

Every Johnson needs his Boswell, but the Victorian Browning required a more discreet and objective biographer than the 18th-century Scotsman to tell his story. In Mrs. Orr and John Nettleship RB found the right judgment, sensitivity and discretion and in them he confided. Mrs. Orr, sister of Frederic Leighton, was widowed young. Intelligent but short-sighted, she found reading difficult and so Browning used to read aloud to her twice a week at her father's house. She was an early member of the Browning Society, with whose encouragement she published her *Handbook* in 1885. After Browning's death his family chose her as Browning's official biographer, so Sarianna filled in those details of Browning's life which he had not already told Mrs. Orr. The result, which displeased the family, was as accurate a portrait of Browning as the selected facts allowed. Mrs. Orr was helped in her *Handbook* by J.T. Nettleship, who had been responsible for the first serious critical account of Browning's work in his *Essays on Robert Browning's Poetry* (1868). Nettleship, who was an animal artist, was only 27 when his shrewd book appeared, and he immediately struck up a working friendship with the poet which lasted until 1889. His book was reprinted, twice its original length, as *Robert Browning: Essays and Thoughts* in 1901.

135. Browning, Robert, *Ferishtah's Fancies*, London, 1884

Presentation copy. RB has annotated the book, clarifying all the proper names and translating Persian quotations. This was to help Mrs. Orr's account of *Ferishtah*, which she included as an appendix to her *Handbook*.

136a. Orr, Mrs. Sutherland, *A Handbook to the Works of Robert Browning*, London, 1885

First edition. This guide to Browning's work was used extensively and went through five editions. On the title-page Mrs. Orr quotes Browning's words 'No pause i' the leading and the light," which gives a slightly hectic appearance to what is a sane and sensible book.

b. Orr, Mrs. Sutherland, *Life and Letters of Robert Browning*, London, 1891

137. Browning, Robert, *Parleyings with Certain People of Importance in Their Day*, London, 1887

Presentation copy to Nettleship. Tipped in is a letter from RB, 21 August 1889, correcting a passage in "Parleyings with Christopher Smart" which Nettleship had criticised. RB also explains a query: "My 'pessimistic friend' was Carlyle—whose words on the subject of his despondency . . . are recorded by Froude. I thought I had distinguished him sufficiently by the mention of his 'guffaw'."

138. Nettleship, J.T., *Essays on Robert Browning's Poetry*, London, 1868

FREDERICK J. FURNIVALL (1825–1910)

F.J. Furnivall, Browning's greatest publicist, with piercing eyes and heavy whiskers, was completely different from the discreet Mrs. Orr and J.T. Nettleship. During the last decade of Browning's life Furnivall did everything in his power to make the poet's works known to as wide a readership as possible. With Emily Hickey, he founded the Browning Society in 1881. Also he wrote a bibliography, and he pestered George Smith to produce a shilling selection of Browning's works. Full of sound and fury, of energy and fire, Furnivall troubled Browning as quarrels and feuds exploded around him. Yet, in spite of the rumpus, Browning couldn't help liking the man. He was first approached by Furnivall in 1872 on Chaucer Society business, and he reluctantly accepted the Presidency of the New Shakspere Society (also formed by Furnivall) in 1879, having refused it five years earlier. He watched the founding of the Browning Society with embarrassed tolerance. Under Furnivall's noisy leadership the Society helped to boost Browning's sales during the 1880's, and they would have been improved still more had Smith adopted Furnivall's suggestion about a cheap edition earlier than he did. After Browning's death Furnivall quarrelled with Sarianna and Pen. The Browning Society collapsed in 1892 and Furnivall directed his attentions elsewhere.

139. Beerbohm, Max, Robert Browning taking tea with the Browning Society, ca. 1903–04

Pencil sketch for a watercolour published in *The Poet's Corner*, 1904. The drawing wittily satirizes the members of the Browning Society—the aesthetes, the scholars and the Victorian middle-class. Browning himself, rather consciously, stirs his tea, wrapt in thought.

140. Browning, Robert, *Dramatis Personae*, Second edition, 1864

Furnivall's copy. He annotated the poems, as was his custom, and stuck in a copy of the Fradelle and Young photograph of Browning circulated to the Browning Society in 1882. Under his signature he recorded the date and time when "Teena" lost her life. Teena Rochfort Smith was Furnivall's young secretary and mistress, who died when her dress accidentally caught fire. Her death and the discovery of the relationship led to the end of Furnivall's marriage. Unsuspecting, RB had been introduced to Teena, and he was later surprised to find his photograph adorning a booklet Furnivall printed in her memory.

THOMAS HARDY (1840–1928)

Browning and Thomas Hardy were little more than nodding acquaintances at London parties. This was hardly surprising—as their backgrounds, personalities and outlook on life were so different. Even so, Hardy owed a great deal to Browning, who was a major influence on his poetry. Hardy's novels, too, are sprinkled with quotations from Browning. Like Henry James, Hardy was puzzled by Browning—"How could smug Christian optimism worthy of a dissenting grocer find a place inside a man who was so vast a seer and feeler when on neutral ground?"

141. Hardy, Thomas, *Wessex Tales*, London, 1888, 2 vols.

Vol. 1, inscribed by Hardy on half-title: "To Robert Browning Esq., D.C.L. from Thomas Hardy. May 1888."

142. Letter from Thomas Hardy to Katharine Bronson, 31 May 1887

Written on his return to England from Italy to thank her for a present. Thomas and Emma Hardy had visited Mrs. Bronson in Venice with an introduction from RB.

Chronology

1806 6 March: EBB born at Coxhoe Hall near Durham, eldest of eleven surviving children of Edward Moulton-Barrett and Mary Graham-Clarke.

9 March: EBB privately baptized by the Revd. William Lewis Rham, Rector of Fersfield, Norfolk, a family friend.

1808 10 February: EBB publicly baptized at Kelloe Church, Co. Durham.

ca. late autumn: Moulton-Barretts move to London.

1809 ca. April: Moulton-Barretts move to North End, Hammersmith.

1810 Moulton-Barretts move to Hope End Estate.

1812 7 May: RB born at Southampton St., Camberwell.

1820 6 March: Probably as a present for her 14th birthday, 50 copies of EBB's first book, *The Battle of Marathon*, privately printed.

1821 May: EBB first appears publicly as a poet when her "Stanzas, Excited by Some Reflections on the Present State of Greece," are published in *The New Monthly Magazine*, Second Series, I, 523.

June: EBB's first serious illness diagnosed as a "nervous disorder" by Dr. Coker, who prescribes opium; the drug induces an addiction that remains with her throughout her life.

July: EBB's "Thoughts Awakened by Contemplating a Piece of the Palm Which Grows on the Summit of the Acropolis at Athens" published in *The New Monthly Magazine*, Second Series, II, 59.

1824 30 June: EBB's "Stanzas on the Death of Lord Byron" published in the London *Globe and Traveller*.

1825 19 November: EBB's "The Rose and Zephyr" published in *The Literary Gazette, and Journal of the Belles Lettres.*

1826 RB leaves the school of Revd. Thomas Martin Ready at Peckham. His education at this establishment, probably for six years, was augmented by his father's instructions. He was also tutored privately in French and Italian. He studied music under John Relfe, Musician-in-Ordinary to the King and a pupil of the Abbé Vogler. During this period RB is profoundly influenced by Shelley; this lasts for several years and leads to periods of atheism and vegetarianism.

25 March: EBB's *An Essay on Mind with Other Poems* published by James Duncan.

6 May: EBB's "Irregular Stanzas" published in *The Literary Gazette, and Journal of the Belles Lettres.*

1827 January: EBB's poem, "Who art thou of the veilëd countenance," published in *The Jewish Expositor and Friend of Israel.*

31 May: Sarah Flower transcribes in her letter to W.J. Fox two early poetical efforts of RB: "The first born of Egypt" and "The Dance of Death."

1828 October: RB enrolls at the newly-formed University of London to study Greek, Latin, and German.

7 October: EBB's mother dies.

1829 May: RB withdraws from London University.

1831 31 May: EBB's "Kings" published in *The Times.*

4 June: EBB commences a diary which records for the next 10 months her anxiety over the anticipated and eventual removal from Hope End.

1832 13 January: EBB's "The Pestilence" published in *The Times.*

23 August: EBB and family leave Hope End and settle at Sidmouth.

22 October: RB conceives the plan of writing a poem, an opera, and a novel under pen names, after leaving Edmund Kean's performance of *Richard III*. This plan leads to the composition of *Pauline*.

1833 March: RB's *Pauline: A Fragment of a Confession* published anonymously by Saunders and Otley.

11 May: EBB's translation of *Prometheus Bound* published by A.J. Valpy.

30 October: RB reads the copy of *Pauline* annotated by John Stuart Mill, a harsh criticism of his morbid self-revelation. Thereafter, RB resolves to write dramatically.

1834 October: RB's sonnet "Eyes calm beside thee (Lady, couldst thou know!)" published in *The Monthly Repository*, signed "Z."

1835 15 August: RB's *Paracelsus* published by Effingham Wilson.

September: EBB's "Stanzas Addressed to Miss Landon, and Suggested by Her 'Stanzas on the Death of Mrs. Hemans'" published in *The New Monthly Magazine*."

November: RB's "A King lived long ago" published in *The Monthly Repository*, signed "Z."

ca. 2 December: EBB and family move to 74 Gloucester Place, London.

1836 January: RB's "Porphyria" and "Johannes Agricola" published in *The Monthly Repository*, both signed "Z."

19 March: EBB's "Man and Nature" published in *The Athenæum*.

May: RB's lines beginning "Still ailing, Wind?" published in *The Monthly Repository*, signed "Z."

July: EBB's "The Romaunt of Margret" published in *The New Monthly Magazine*.

2 July: EBB's "The Seaside Walk" published in *The Athenæum*.

23 July: EBB's "A Thought on Thoughts" published in *The Athenæum*.

October: EBB's "The Poet's Vow" published in *The New Monthly Magazine*.

1837 January: EBB's "The Island" published in *The New Monthly Magazine*.

1 May: RB's *Strafford: An Historical Tragedy* published by Longmans; opens at Covent Garden; closes after four performances.

1 July: EBB's "The Young Queen" published in *The Athenæum*.

8 July: EBB's "Victoria's Tears" published in *The Athenæum*.

1838 EBB's "A Romance of the Ganges" published in *Findens' Tableaux*.

mid-April: EBB moves to 50 Wimpole Street.

6 June: EBB's *The Seraphim, and Other Poems* published by Saunders and Otley.

August: Under medical advice, to recuperate from a lung hemorrhage, EBB moves to Torquay.

1839 EBB's "The Romaunt of the Page" published in *Findens' Tableaux*.

EBB's "A Sabbath on the Sea" published in *The Amaranth*.

26 January: EBB's "L.E.L.'s Last Question" published in *The Athenæum*.

1840 EBB's "The Dream" and "The Legend of the Brown Rosarie" published in *Findens' Tableaux*.

15 February: EBB's "The Crowned and Wedded Queen" published in *The Athenæum*.

29 February: The announced date of publication of RB's *Sordello*, which was actually published the following week by Edward Moxon.

April: EBB's "A Night Watch by the Sea" published in *The Monthly Chronicle*.

July: EBB's "A Joy of the Rose" published in *The Monthly Chronicle*.

4 July: EBB's "Napoleon's Return" published in *The Athenæum*.

11 July: EBB's brother Edward drowns in a sailing accident in Tor Bay. She suffers a near-fatal illness as a result.

late December: RB's family moves from Camberwell to New Cross, Hatcham, in Surrey.

1841 April: RB's *Pippa Passes* (*Bells and Pomegranates, No. I*) published by Edward Moxon.

September: EBB returns to Wimpole Street.

1842 EBB writes critical series on the English Poets for *The Athenæum*; collaborates with Mary Russell Mitford on *Bijou Almanack*.

March: RB's *King Victor and King Charles* (*Bells and Pomegranates, No. II*) published by Edward Moxon.

November: RB's *Dramatic Lyrics* (*Bells and Pomegranates, No. III*) published by Edward Moxon.

1843 EBB collaborates with R.H. Horne on *A New Spirit of the Age* (1844).

January: RB's *The Return of the Druses* (*Bells and Pomegranates, No. IV*) published by Edward Moxon.

11 February: RB's *A Blot in the 'Scutcheon* (*Bells and Pomegranates, No. V*) published by Edward Moxon; it opens at the Drury Lane Theatre and closes after three performances.

1844 20 April: RB's *Colombe's Birthday* (*Bells and Pomegranates, No. VI*) published by Edward Moxon.

14 August: EBB's *Poems* (1844) published by Edward Moxon.

1845 10 January: RB writes first letter to EBB.

20 May: First meeting of RB and EBB at Wimpole Street.

6 November: RB's *Dramatic Romances and Lyrics* (*Bells and Pomegranates, No. VII*) published by Edward Moxon.

1846 13 April: RB's *Luria* and *A Soul's Tragedy* (*Bells and Pomegranates, No. VIII*) published by Edward Moxon.

12 September: RB and EBB marry in St. Marylebone Church, London; only two witnesses are present.

19 September: RB and EBB leave London for Italy, settling in Pisa.

1847 April: Brownings settle in Florence, Italy.

1848 Brownings make their permanent home in Casa Guidi.

1849 RB's *Poems* published in two volumes.

9 March: Birth at Casa Guidi of Robert Wiedemann Barrett Browning, called Penini, or Pen for short.

18 March: RB's mother dies.

1850 1 April: RB's *Christmas-Eve and Easter-Day* published by Chapman & Hall; first book, apart from *Strafford*, brought out at publisher's expense.

1 November: EBB's *Poems* (1850) published by Chapman & Hall; includes first appearance of "Sonnets from the Portuguese."

1851 31 May: EBB's *Casa Guidi Windows* published by Chapman & Hall.

1852 RB's "An Essay on Shelley" published by Edward Moxon as an introduction to a volume of Shelley's letters, which later proved spurious.

1853 12 October: EBB's *Poems* (1853) published by Chapman & Hall.

1854 April: RB & EBB's *Two Poems* published by Bradbury and Evans.

1855 10 January: EBB's correspondent and longtime friend, Mary Russell Mitford, dies.

17 November: RB's *Men and Women* published by Chapman & Hall.

1856 1 November: EBB's *Poems* (1856) published by Chapman & Hall.

3 December: John Kenyon, close friend and benefactor of the Brownings for many years, dies leaving £4,500 to EBB; £6,500 to RB.

1857 EBB's *Aurora Leigh* published by Chapman & Hall.

17 April: EBB's father dies.

1860 12 March: EBB's *Poems Before Congress* published by Chapman & Hall.

June: RB purchases the Old Yellow Book in a Florence book stall.

1861 29 June: EBB dies at Casa Guidi; buried in Protestant Cemetery 1 July.

July: RB commissions George Mignaty to paint a picture of the Drawing Room at Casa Guidi.

1 August: RB leaves Florence.

October: RB arrives in England; establishes permanent residence, the following May, at 19 Warwick Crescent, London.

1862 20 March: EBB's *Last Poems* published by Chapman & Hall.

1863 RB's *The Poetical Works* published in three volumes.

1864 28 May: RB's *Dramatis Personae* published by Chapman & Hall.

1866 20 June: RB's father dies in Paris.

1867 26 June: RB receives honorary degree of M.A. from Oxford University.

1868 RB's *The Poetical Works* published in six volumes by Smith, Elder & Co.

21 November: RB's *The Ring and the Book*, vol. i, published by Smith, Elder & Co.

26 December: RB's *The Ring and the Book*, vol. ii, published by Smith, Elder & Co.

1869 30 January: RB's *The Ring and the Book*, vol. iii, published by Smith, Elder & Co.

27 February: RB's *The Ring and the Book*, vol. iv, published by Smith, Elder & Co.

1871 8 August: RB's *Balaustion's Adventure, Including a Transcript from Euripides* published by Smith, Elder & Co.

16 December: RB's *Prince Hohenstiel-Schwangau, Saviour of Society* published by Smith, Elder & Co.

1872 4 June: RB's *Fifine at the Fair* published by Smith, Elder & Co.

1873 early May: RB's *Red Cotton Night-Cap Country, or Turf and Towers* published by Smith, Elder & Co.

1875 15 April: RB's *Aristophanes' Apology* published by Smith, Elder & Co.

late November: RB's *The Inn Album* published by Smith, Elder & Co.

1876 18 July: RB's *Of Pacchiarotto and How He Worked in Distemper* published by Smith, Elder & Co.

1877 15 October: RB's *The Agamemnon of Æschylus* published by Smith, Elder & Co.

1878 15 May: RB's *La Saisiaz* and *The Two Poets of Croisic* published in one volume by Smith, Elder & Co.

1879 28 April: RB's *Dramatic Idyls* [first series] published by Smith, Elder & Co.

1880 15 June: RB's *Dramatic Idyls, Second Series* published by Smith, Elder & Co.

1881 October: Founding of the London Browning Society by F.J. Furnivall and Emily Hickey.

1882 14 June: RB receives honorary degree of D.C.L. from Oxford University.

1883 9 March: RB's *Jocoseria* published by Smith, Elder & Co.

8 December: RB's "Goldoni" published in the *Pall Mall Gazette*.

28 December: RB's "Helen's Tower" published in the *Pall Mall Gazette*.

1884 February: RB's "Rawdon Brown" published in *Century Magazine*.

21 November: RB's *Ferishtah's Fancies* published by Smith, Elder & Co.

1887 28 January: RB's *Parleyings with Certain People of Importance in Their Day* published by Smith, Elder & Co.

4 October: Pen Browning marries Fannie Coddington.

16 October: RB removes to 29 De Vere Gardens.

1889 13 July: RB's "To Edward FitzGerald" published in *The Athenæum*.

12 December: RB dies in Venice; *Asolando: Fancies and Facts* published by Smith, Elder & Co.

31 December: RB is buried in Westminster Abbey.

1912 8 July: Pen Browning dies at Asolo, Italy.

1913 1–8 May: The Browning Collections sold at auction by Messrs. Sotheby, Wilkinson & Hodge.

Lenders To The Exhibition

Mary V. Altham, Babbacombe, England, 4a, 41b, 53b, 55a

R.J.L. Altham, London, 6, 46a, 72b

Armstrong Browning Library, Baylor University, Waco, Texas, 5, 9, 14, 15, 16, 17, 19a, 20, 26, 29b, 32a, 32b, 34, 35b, 35c, 36b, 38, 40a, 40c, 41a, 43, 47a, 47c, 47d, 47e, 48a, 48b, 48c, 50b, 51a, 51b, 51c, 51d, 51e, 51f, 52a, 52b, 52c, 52d, 55b, 56, 58b, 59, 60b, 66, 67, 68a, 69, 70, 71b, 76, 77, 78, 79a, 79b, 80, 81a, 81b, 83a, 83c, 83d, 83e, 84a, 85a, 85b, 85c, 85e, 86b, 86c, 88d, 89a, 89d, 90a, 90d, 90e, 91a, 91b, 91c, 91e, 92, 94, 96, 97, 101, 102a, 104, 105, 106, 108, 109, 110, 111, 113, 114, 116, 117, 118, 122b, 123, 128, 129b, 132b, 133, 134, 136a, 136b, 138, 139

Master and Fellows of Balliol College, Oxford, England, 65a, 72c, 87b, 87c, 127, 135

The Henry W. & Albert A. Berg Collection, The New York Public Library, Astor, Lenox and Tilden Foundations, New York, 120a

Roy E. Bolton, London, 68b

Special Collections, Mugar Memorial Library, Boston University, Boston, Massachusetts, 119

Special Collections, Harold B. Lee Library, Brigham Young University, Provo, Utah, 21, 24

Special Collections, The John Hay Library, Brown University, Providence, Rhode Island, 73

The Browning Institute, New York, 35a, 40b, 42, 46c, 54, 74a, 74b, 115

The Browning Settlement, London, 22

The Browning Society of London, 47b

Joel Tanner Hart Papers, Reuben T. Durrett Collection, Department of Special Collections, University of Chicago, Chicago, Illinois, 57

Special Collections, Colby College, Waterville, Maine, 141

Special Collections, Butler Library, Columbia University, New York, 120b
Library of Congress, Washington, D.C., 90b
Mr. & Mrs. Harry L. Dalton, Charlotte, North Carolina, 29a
Provost and Fellows of Eton College, Windsor, England, 88a, 93, 142
Joseph Francus, Baltimore, Maryland, 36a
Philip Kelley, Winfield, Kansas, 23, 37, 40d, 58c, 84e, 85b, 87d, 88c, 112
Katharine Macdonald, London, 86a
Michael Francis McGraw, 36a
Michael Meredith, Eton, England, 13, 18, 33a, 58a, 63, 84d, 85d, 86d, 87d, 100, 103, 126, 132a, 140
Albert M. Bender Collection, Mills College, Oakland, California, 49b, 50a, 61
Edward R. Moulton-Barrett, Platt, England, 1, 3, 4b, 8, 10a, 10b, 10c, 11a, 11b, 12a, 12b, 25a, 25b, 39, 48d, 53a, 72a, 75, 82b, 95, 98, 131
Gordon E. Moulton-Barrett, Miami, Florida, 2, 28a
Ohio Wesleyan University, Delaware, Ohio, 46b, 60a, 87e
Frank Patenella, 36a
R.H. Taylor Collection, Princeton University, Princeton, New Jersey, 83b, 87a, 89b
Gordon N. Ray, New York, 45, 84b, 102b, 124
University of Reading, Reading, England, 137
Mark Samuels Lasner, Charlottesville, Virginia, 49a, 83f, 84c
The Browning Collection, Scripps College, Claremont, California, 30, 31b, 44, 65b, 72d, 72e, 99
Sutro Library, San Francisco, California, 48e
The George Arents Research Library for Special Collections, University of Syracuse, New York, 31a, 33b, 71a, 121, 125, 129a
Harry Ransom Humanities Research Center, University of Texas at Austin, 82a, 107, 122a, 130
The English Poetry Collection, Wellesley College Library, Wellesley, Massachusetts, 27, 28b, 28c, 28d, 88b, 90c, 91d
Department of Archives, Marylebone Library, City of Westminster, London, 7
Edwin Wolf, II, Philadelphia, Pennsylvania, 62
Robert B. Wolf, Philadelphia, Pennsylvania, 89c
Provost and Fellows of Worcester College, Oxford, England, 64
A.W. Yeats, Beaumont, Texas, 19b

About The Author

Michael Meredith, graduate of Balliol College, Oxford, is a member of the English Department at Eton College. He has an extensive personal Browning collection and is President of the Browning Society of London. Meredith has written previously on both Robert and Elizabeth Barrett Browning and recently edited *More Than Friend* (1985), the correspondence between Robert Browning and Katharine Bronson. He is currently working on a Browning bibliography and on a study of Browning's *Asolando*.